25 WAYS MOMS can Raise Extraordinary KIDS

STACIA PIERCE

1st Printing

25 Ways Moms Can Raise Extraordinary Kids

ISBN: 1-886-880-22-0
Copyright © 1999 by Stacia Pierce
Published by Life Changers Publishing
808 Lake Lansing Rd. Ste. 200
East Lansing, MI 48823

Table of Contents

DEDICATION
ACKNOWLEDGMENTS
INTRODUCTION

Part I Learn

Part II: Love

Part III: Laugh

DEDICATION

To my mother Phyllis Scott, who believed in my dreams, exposed me to greatness, prayed for me to stay on course and fulfill my purpose, and who still serves as a continual source of inspiration to me in writing books.

ACKNOWLEDGMENTS

Special thanks to: Sabrina Todd, Cathy Wray, Sharlette Marshall, Ruth Reed and Daphine Whitfield for their valued assistance in writing this book.

INTRODUCTION

A few of the chapters have been written by Cathy Wray and Sabrina Todd with final editing done by me. Both women have been trained and mentored by me and are members of my staff and women's leadership team. All of our children are in different age groups and I wanted you, to have a full scope on how to raise children from infants to teens. I am proud to say that these ladies have taken heed to my pastoral teachings and are excellent moms.

I hope you find within these pages the inspiration you need to raise positive, extraordinary kids. I Prepared this book to be an easy read with simple solutions and practical principles that when applied will lead to success.

Finally, I hope that I achieved my goal in writing this book by turning you the reader into a motivated mom!

1 Wake Up Your Child's Dreams

"Most men die from the neck up because they stop dreaming."
- Ben Franklin

From my childhood I have learned how important atmosphere is in the dream process. I can recall my father nudging me to think about my future and plan big. He provided the tools and the atmosphere that caused me to be a dreamer. Because of his influence, I have always tried to create the right home environment for our entire family.

A few years ago, when my husband and I went looking for a new home, I wanted a home where our family dreams would come true. I chose the house we currently live in because it has lots of windows in every room and the sun shines in perfectly; the carpet is bright and the basement is finished and cozy. The bathrooms are beautiful and the backyard is big.

Although this is not our final destination, I know that during my children's growing years, the location and atmosphere they grow up in is important to their development. When we walked through the house with the previous owners the wife commented to me, "This is a happy house. We've had lots of fun memories." Those words sold me because it was confirmation of what I was

13

looking for in a home. You don't have to move into a new home, but do create an environment of excellence wherever you live. Your children's creative genius can be dimmed or worse yet robbed, if placed in a dense, uncaring atmosphere that doesn't give them a chance to develop.

Helping your children to dream and live their dream out is so rewarding to a parent. Our son Ryan is approaching two years old and he's beginning to explore the world around him. He's too young to create a dream list, but it's perfect time for me to begin stimulating his imagination. I provided him with paper, markers, crayons, paints and colored pencils to stir his artistic expression. For both of my children I have carved out a creative corner in our home for them. It's important to provide a child with a place to escape the pressures and inhibitions of school.

Set up creative play space separate from where your child does homework and keep it stocked with costumes, crayons, paint, paper, colored markers, glue, clay and other creative accessories. Keep this creative corner set up and it will serve as a constant invitation to your children to sit down and dream-up new creations all their own. Since my daughter is getting a little older, I have provided her with a notebook and sketch pad where she can journalize and draw. The latest creative tool I bought her was a *Doodle a Day Calendar by American Girl*. When you provide this type of atmosphere you are nurturing curiosity, and it offers your children many opportunities for discovery.

14

In order to wake up your child's dreams, they'll need supervision and positive direction. Every year since my daughter was six, I've had her develop a dream list right before the new year begins. It's amazing to see how their dreams develop and how encouraged a child can become when their dreams are realized.

"The future belongs to those who believe in the beauty of their dreams"

I believe it is an act of love for me to be involved in my child's dreams. It demonstrates that I believe in them and that what's important to them is important to me. The dream list helps me get involved. One of Ariana's dreams on her dream list is to write a book. Consistently I encourage her to start writing now. I buy her published books by children authors. As parents we have to get involved in the activities that our children partake in.

At six years old , my daughter had on her dream list that she wanted to be a cheerleader. For two years she cut out pictures and posted them on poster board and read about cheerleading. Now two years later at age eight, she is on a cheerleading squad, and cheers at most of the local parades. You may be raising a future Olympic gold medalist, a famous inventor or a world renown artist, so take your children's dreams seriously. Encouraging our children to think about big things causes them to soar in their confidence and to believe they can achieve.

Give Your Child Options

Open your children up to life expanding options. Both Ryan and Ariana love going to museums, only because I exposed them to the pleasure of visiting museums at a young age. Visit libraries, travel, have lunch at a tea room, and frequent festivals. Go to concerts, symphonies and plays. With lots of options your children will be better able to define what interests them. As a family we usually see at least four Broadway plays a year. Ryan, who just turned two, recently experienced his first Broadway play, *Beauty & the Beast.* He behaved pretty good for attending his first live performance.

Dream Building Days

From time to time Ariana and her friends gather at our home for a dream-building day. They bring their Story Books my new Prayer and Purpose Planners for boys and girls.

The children engage in cutting pictures from magazines, gluing them in their book and decorating their pages with stickers, stamps and fun drawings. This activity causes the children to frame their future with faith photos.

Discover Your Children's Interests

It's almost essential that you have a home computer today, especially since most kids have access to one at school. But even simple activities like working on the computer, gardening, becoming a boy or girl scout and taking music lessons can wake up your child's dreams. When we allow our children to explore unknown areas of interest, they discover their strengths and weaknesses, their likes and dislikes and may even stumble upon something meaningful.

Church and Your Child's Dream

Although your home is an essential part of their dream building, church is the most important dream building environment. A good church will aid your children in reaching their dreams.

We always stress to our children that attending church is a priority for a successful life. Church activities are important to dream building because it teaches children to know that God is an important part of their life. Children should also be taught to pray about their dreams and give God a chance to get involved in their personal circumstances. For me as I young adult, it wasn't until I got plugged into a good church that I ever had the faith to believe in my dreams.

Communication

The way you communicate with your children will determine how they dream. Your children need positive feedback from you. Your home should be a place where they can get affirmation, support, and encouragement. Saying things like, "That's a  crazy idea; that's stupid; cant' you think?" or "Where's your head?" will paralyze your child's dreams. As a parent, you have to get your self-esteem intact so you can be a positive influence in your child's life. If your children do not get encouragement from you, then they'll hold back from sharing anything with you. During those times of intimate sharing we discover what our children's real interests are.

You show encouragement with both words and actions. Studies have proven that in general, most parents don't help children with homework, talk with them daily about school issues, take their kids to the library, or plan individual time with each child. It's no wonder most children today say they have no future dreams. Every child needs at least one adult who believes in them and their dreams. Become that one adult! Have your child compose a dream list, and then share it with you. This is sample of my daughter Ariana's list.

Ariana'a Dream List 1999

1. Sing
2. Write a book
3. Learn to draw well
4. Get good grades in school
5. Adopt a teenager
6. Go to a good college
7. Move into a mansion
8. Get braces quickly
9. Move in with my friends when I'm in college
10. Get a computer
11. Be healthy and run fast
12. Read a lot more
13. Continue to have a happy life and family
14. Pray everyday and night
15. Have a good vacation (New York)

 **Idea File**

🔔 GIVE EACH AGE APPROPRIATE CHILD A BLANK PIECE OF PAPER NUMBERED FROM 1-10 AND ASK THEM TO CREATE A DREAM LIST OF THINGS THEY WANT TO DO, SEE, AND HAVE.

🔔 MAKE A LIST OF PLACES YOU CAN TAKE YOUR CHILDREN TO GIVE THEM OPTIONS TO DISCOVER THEIR DREAMS.

Create a Talent Portfolio to Develop Your Child's Dream

"Talent portfolios give your child a reference to mark their ability to see their dreams come true."

-Darice Marshall

Every child is born with some sort of giftedness, or a talent that could later grow into a rewarding career. Nurturing that talent is important. You have to help your children unbury the treasures within them.

As parents we should help our children figure out who they are. One of the most important things a parent can do for a child is to help that child figure out his or her pattern of strengths and weaknesses. What matters most are those things a child can turn into a lifelong pursuit. For example, when I was a child I loved fashion, modeling, taking personal improvement classes, charm courses and helping other girls my age feel better about themselves. I can easily remember my first charm course, at a church my family attended. I was eight years old and the pastor's wife taught an eight week charm course to all of the young ladies. It impacted my life so much that I continually wanted more books and information on the subject long after the course was over.

My school didn't really have any subjects that would cause this talent to be recognized, but my parents made an awesome investment in me by sending me to modeling schools and paying

21

for charm courses. Today I turned that interest into a lifelong career motivating and leading women to pursue their purpose and hosting major women's conferences. My life is so fulfilling and rewarding and I believe it's because I was in touch with my unique talents long ago. As a parent you can ask God for help in recognizing your kids talents. I pray over both my children and I ask God to help me make the right choices on what to get my children involved in. I pray that God helps me to discover those things they have a passion for and give me the wisdom to be able to properly support them.

How To Create A Talent Portfolio

1. Buy a three ring binder with a slip cover jacket and make a cover for each child. You could have each child design their own cover as well.

2. Creating a portfolio is simple. Sit down with your children to discuss and write down their favorite activities, academic or otherwise, abilities and interests as well as what they like or dislike about different learning situations. Use topic headings to get your child started in developing his or her portfolio. You may want to share the completed notebook with your child's teacher so she can understand more about your child. Then have your child record:

3. The subjects "I like or I'm good at."

4. Activities , clubs, lessons I enjoy outside of school

5. The projects I like to work on at home

6. Family activities and special experiences I enjoy

7. How I learn best. (In my room, at the kitchen table, with soft music playing, in the morning, in the afternoon with lots of lights, etc.)

8. Ways I like to show what I'm learning. (discussion or writing)

9. My goals

10. My dreams

11. Ways I think best (creative, inventive, in school)

Idea File

ONCE YOU HAVE ALL THE IMPORTANT INFORMATION IN YOUR TALENT PORTFOLIO, BEGIN TO COLLECT CERTIFICATES OF ACHIEVEMENT, ART WORK, AND BOOK REPORTS. PUT PICTURES OF YOUR CHILDREN IN ACTION DOING ACTIVITIES THEY REALLY ENJOY. PERIODICALLY GO THROUGH THE TALENT PORTFOLIO WITH YOUR CHILD AND DISCUSS THEIR INTERESTS. OLDER CHILDREN CAN KEEP UP WITH THEIR OWN PORTFOLIOS. YOU WILL BEGIN TO SEE A COMMON THREAD WEAVED THROUGHOUT YOUR CHILD'S PORTFOLIO, WHICH WILL GIVE YOU CLUES CONCERNING THEIR TALENT AND CALL IN LIFE.

⊕ WRITE DOWN WHAT TALENTS OR GIFTS YOU HAVE NOTICED IN EACH OF YOUR CHILDREN. DON'T OVERLOOK ANYTHING. FOR EXAMPLE, YOUR KIDS MAY HAVE A GIFT OF MERCY, COMPASSION, MOTIVATION OR GIVING. RECORD THESE AS WELL.

3 Expose Your Kids To Greatness

"You can determine where a person is going to be in the next five years by the books he reads, the tapes he listens to and the people he hangs around."

- Charles "Tremendous" Jones

My children's life goals have greatly expanded by exposing them to some very successful people. My husband and I have hosted some major conferences and events with some of the most successful men and women in our society. Many of them have been special guests in our home and my children have come to know and admire them.

We have never allowed any of our guests to treat our kids as though they were nonexistent or unimportant. Instead we make sure that we introduce them and allow our children an opportunity to speak and interact with them, if the circumstances permit it.

We don't send our kids to bed every time guests come over; sometimes we include them in the visit. I discovered from reading how royal families and the affluent raise their children that they demand respect for their children from their peers and protegees. As the parent, you have to set the standards for the way people will treat your kids, but first you must deem them as special. You cannot expect others to treat your kids in a way that you are not willing to treat them yourself. Two of my daughter's favorite recording artists are Angelo & Veronica, who are very good friends of ours. The first time they came to our church they autographed a picture for Ariana. They wrote, "Ariana, you are such a beautiful and smart girl; you'll do great things." Those words stayed with her and she was motivated by them because she admired them. We have also had them in our home which has made a lasting impact on her.

Ariana also got the chance to meet the group Virtue, when my husband and I hosted them one year for our singles conference. After her experience with Virtue, she put on her goal list that she wanted to be a singer. Some other people that have impacted our

daughter are our friends Skot and Barb Welch. They have started one of the first African American owned direct sales and marketing companies. They are extraordinary business people. Every time they are around they make a positive impact on our children. They always take a special interest in our kids by asking them questions concerning the things that they are involved in. The exposure has caused my daughter's interest in entrepreneurship to be peaked. We have engaged in several leisure activities with great recording artists, ministers, athletes, and actors. This exposes our kids to seeing these great people enjoying life and engaging in normal activities. At this point you may be thinking, that's great for you Stacia, but I don't know people like that. There are many influential people who could make a positive impact on your kids. Take them to an author's book signing or introduce them to a friend you have that is a business owner. Once my husband and I began to fulfill our God given purpose in life, people wanted to meet us. So the doors of opportunity naturally opened to expose our kids to great people. I believe the same will happen for you!

7 Ways to Expose Your Kids to Greatness:

1. GET IN THE PRESENCE OF GREAT PEOPLE

At a very young age my father exposed me to great people by taking me with him to motivational seminars and training conferences. I heard some of America's greatest speakers when I was just a teenager. My dad is in the real estate business, and by taking me with him to do business, I met some of the wealthiest real estate agents and entrepreneurs around. I recall vividly having dinner and fishing on the private lake of one of my father's clients, a very wealthy family who owned a Christmas tree business. My father negotiated some very successful deals for the gentleman. As a way of thanking him, he invited our family over to relax with his family for a day. What a life changing experience. It changed my perspective concerning my future. Great people will expand your kids' vision for life.

2. VISIT GREAT STORES

Even if you don't make a purchase, the exposure to a great store allows your kids to see the possibilities of their future. This could also be a great time to teach a lesson about finances. Explain to them how much money it takes to buy nice things. Last summer while on vacation in New York, we took the kids to FAO Swartz toy store on Fifth Avenue, which is one of the biggest toy stores in America. Ariana was amazed at all of the choices. We did buy several toys for her and Ryan, but most of all she appreciated just seeing the store.

Nike Town shoe store in Chicago is another great store, especially if your kids are into sports. We try to visit there are least once a year. There is a new American Girls store for girls in Chicago. If your daughter likes *American Girl* magazine, she'll love the store. It has a restaurant, photo studio, clothes and dolls. Great stores will expose your kids to excellent products and allows them to know what's available to them.

3. GO TO GREAT PLACES

Try taking your girls to an authentic tea room for lunch. Both of you get all dressed up and enjoy a mother/daughter day together. Recently, Ariana and I had this experience and it was so special. Take your boys to a professional baseball, basketball or football game. A family trip to the Olympics would expose the entire family to great athletes.

4. Eat at Great Restaurants

Add fine dining to your list of family outings. Your kids will learn restaurant etiquette at a young age if you take them to a five star restaurant on occasion. Go to one where you must be dressed up. Have them order something new, not just a burger.

5. See Great Homes

Every year we try to take the family to the Parade of Homes to get decorating ideas and plan for our next home. You can't think bigger until you are exposed to bigger. Occasionally drive through the neighborhood with your kids where you would like your next home to be so your children will have a faith photo of their future.

Sometimes visual illustrations are the best teaching methods. Drive your children through an impoverished neighborhood to allow them to see how some people live. Then explain to them how they would have to live that way if you spent all of your money and did not save any. Also explain to them how hard work and determination is the key to having nice things. By exposing your kids to greatness, you stretch them to do great things themselves.

6. Visit Great Churches

Church is a very intricate part of our life. My husband and I are called to build a successful church. Consequently, we want our children to grow up in a church they can be proud of. Our corporate mission is to build a great church that will impact thousands of people and radically change ordinary people into extraordinary people by the word of God. Therefore we took our children to visit some of the greatest churches in America. We went on tours, acquired information and even attended services there. The exposure to great churches allowed our children and my husband and I to get a visual image of the kind of ministry we would build together. Also, it allowed our family to see that God does great things through men and women of God who serve Him and have a big vision.

Before you choose a church to join, I suggest that you take into consideration something other than your own needs- the needs of your children. Think ahead to the future. Even if your children are young, look into the youth program at the church. Do they have one? Is it on it's way? Will it be the kind of teaching your kids need? Once your child has developed relationships at the church, you won't want to change churches just to find a good youth program. We have put a lot into our children's and youth ministries so that our children can grow up full of faith. They are taught the word of God on their level.

In our youth program, many of the kids age fourteen to eighteen years old are bused to church without their parents. It has amazed me how parents want their kids to grow up with righteous morals and a godly character, but won't make the necessary changes in their own life to support what they want. Once you find a good church commit to it. To raise extraordinary children, get involved in a extraordinary church yourself.

7. CHOOSE GREAT TEACHERS

I agree with Mark Hansen who said, "Audit your children's teachers." Choose only great and inspiring teachers for your sons and daughters. Every subject can be illuminated by a great and inspiring teacher. Every year I pray that my daughter has a great teacher who will celebrate her, not tolerate her. But I also watch to see how Ariana is responding to her teachers and if her teachers have her best interest at heart. At the time of this writing my daughter's teacher is exceptionally good; she's extraordinary.

 **Idea File**

WHAT CAN YOU DO THIS WEEK TO EXPOSE YOUR KIDS TO GREATNESS? PLAN TO DO ONE THING AND WATCH YOUR KID'S RESPONSE. WHEN YOU EXPOSE YOUR KIDS TO GREATNESS, ALWAYS DISCUSS THE EXPERIENCE WITH YOUR KIDS.

4 Develop a Personal Growth Plan

"If we succeed in giving the love of learning, the learning itself is sure to follow."

- John Lubbock

Do you want your kids to be brimming with excitement about reading a new book and eager to learn something new? It's possible. Read on to discover how to develop a personal growth program that will change your kids' life.

First you as a Mom must be on a personal growth program before you can enlist your children in one. A consistent, organized personal growth program will have a lasting impression on a child's life. The whole process of personal growth started for me as a kid. My father believed in home education and personal growth. He practiced it and encouraged his kids to do the same. My father would have me look up words in the dictionary and practice the word and meaning for a week. Then he would take me on weekend book excursions to the book store and I would choose several books to read. I loved these weekends with my father because we were never in a rush. We would linger in a bookstore for hours some days. My dad had a follow-up plan as well. A few weeks after purchasing my new books he would say, "So tell me about that book." And eager to share I would make sure I had read the book so I could elaborate.

In my teenage years my dad would give me books to read. I remember him giving me the *Richest Man in Babylon* by George S. Clayson and *How to Win Friends and Influence People* by Dale Carnegie. My dad had took the Dale Carnagie course and was sold on it being a must for success in life. My parents would also monitor what I read. I couldn't just choose any type of book I wanted, I had to have their approval.

 These extraordinary family principles that my parents instilled in me not only caused me to achieve extraordinary success at a young age, but gave me a head start when it came to raising my own children. My daughter will be turning nine years old next month at the time of this writing, and I'm about to adjust her personal growth program. My goal is to boost her curiosity and motivation for self-education. Sir Walter Scott was onto something when he said, ***"All men who have turned out worth anything have had a chief hand in their own education"***.

9 Ways To Develop A Personal Growth Program

1. GATHER TOOLS

I made a colorful package for my daughter called, "tools for achievement." Included in her package was everything she needed for her personal growth program. You could put together this simple kit for your children and entice them to learn.

TOOLS NEEDED:

* Colorful file box with hanging file folders
* Scissors
* 3 hole punch
* 3 ring binder with cover pocket
* Clear plastic sheet protectors
* Gluesticks
* Stapler
* Stickers

Once you gather the tools and present them to your kids, they will immediately know that personal growth is important to you because you made an investment. These tools are for boys as well as girls. You may have to make some adjustments in the products you choose, but everyone needs to gather information and file it.

2. GET YOUR CHILDREN THEIR OWN ADDRESS BOOK

Teach them to gather important information about their friends and organize it. This will be the beginning of your children's networking skills. They'll be able to write letters to friends occasionally to keep in touch. I'm helping her to gather important information about her friends and organize it. Then she can write them occasionally to keep in touch. My daughter has a friend named Alexis who lives about an hour from us, so they correspond by letter. Ariana knows her friend is very entrepreneurial minded. Therefore, Ariana tries to find books or tools that will enhance her business. Alexis does the same for Ariana. For example, for Christmas she sent a beautiful box of stationary to contribute to Ariana's love of writing letters.

Ariana collects information she feels will be helpful to her friends and puts it into her Friends Idea File. Then when she writes a letter she can send them the information. I've taught her that this is how you care for your network. Once you provide your kids with the proper tools for personal growth oftentimes the excitement will manifest and they will want to use them.

3. CLIP, FILE, SAVE

Help your kids choose 3-5 topics that interest them. Label their file folders with these topics. One of the best ways to motivate children is to offer them an opportunity to learn in their areas of interest. You can even use their area of interest to teach them a moral lesson. If a child likes racing cars, for instance, and you want to teach them about honesty, find an honest race car driver, and look for race car stories that support your moral message. Then get magazines, books, and brochures on race cars and have your child clip information that's inspiring to him and have him put it in his Purpose Files and save it.

In essence what you are doing is causing your child to become an expert on his or her subjects of interest. When your child's teacher allows them to do a book report on their topic of choice, have them choose a topic from their Purpose Files. They should get a A+ on the report because after all, they are an expert. I subscribe to magazines that support my kids' interests so they have a consistent and current flow of information available to them. Gather and keep all brochures, pamphlets or handouts that support any of your children's topics of interest.

4. Buy Books for Personal Growth

Take book store trips together. Going to the library is a great alternative, but you want to also fill your house with books of your own. So develop your own library. I agree with John Ruskin who said, "If a book is worth reading, it is worth buying."

Once I discovered what my kids' interests were then I began to research children's books and steer them in the direction of what I wanted them to read. Ariana says I choose "cool" books. As a parent you can find books that your child will be interested in. Oftentimes I choose books that may not be on my child's list of favorite interests, but that will develop them in character and biblical literacy.

5. Set up a daily or weekly reading time.

For example in our house, each child reads thirty minutes each day. My son has books read to him. But Ariana reads on her own. When you create personal growth routines, independent learning becomes a part of your child's lifestyle. It's also wise to have your children read one book at a time until it's finished instead of jumping from book to book. That way they are better able to grasp what they are reading, and they'll experience a sense of accomplishment when they've finished a book.

You can make a reading chart for each child to document their progress. Book reports are another effective way to enhance your child's reading experience.

6. PAY YOUR KIDS TO LEARN

On a weekly basis or on a monthly basis give your children extra allowance for sticking to their personal growth plan. If you pay your kids to learn they will know that you truly value learning. The older children will really be motivated by this program. No matter how old your kids are, it's never too late to start.

7. CREATE A PERSONAL GROWTH SPOT

Once you've designed a growth plan you won't want to turn your kids loose to do as they please. In the beginning your help and input will be necessary to help them become disciplined to learning. Start by designing their growth spot, the location where they will go to read, listen to tapes and learn. I use the children's bedrooms as their growth spots because they're quiet, no televisions are in them, they have proper lighting and all their personal growth tools are easily accessible. For Christmas this year I bought Ariana a personal growth chair. It's the new colorful furniture you blow up. This helps to make her spot inviting. You also will want to set up a daily personal growth time. After dinner is usually the time we use for personal growth.

8. TAKE PERSONAL GROWTH TRIPS

Reinforce your child's learning with visuals. Take outings to zoo's, gardens, hands-on museums, science museums, and history museums. Take them to art galleries, tea rooms or live performances if they are excited about the performing arts. Attending a specialized camp or taking a course or workshop is a great chance for young people to get hands on experience in whatever their interest is in. Last year my daughter attended soccer camp and cheerleading camp. Those were the two sports she was interested in.

9. DESIGN A SPIRITUAL GROWTH PLAN

You don't have to be a Bible expert to teach spiritual growth. Show your kids Bible videos and read Bible stories to them. For older kids provide them with their own bibles, a study notebook and a daily Bible devotional. The Bible on cassette tape is good for bedtime listening. I like the *New Adventure Study Bible*. It's the NIV version by Zondervan for kids ages 6 and up. I've used the *One Year Bible for Kids*, New Living translation by Tyndale House. It has 365 daily readings. *My Faith Journals* for boys and girls by Tommy Nelson Publishing are excellent spiritual journals for growth for children ages 6-10.

Spend some time with your children in a Christian book store or in your church book store looking at books and discovering what appeals to your kids. Next, set up a spiritual growth schedule. For instance, have prayer time every morning or evening. Set aside a Bible reading time, or give a weekly verse to meditate on and discuss with the entire family at the end of the week.

The foundation of your child's spiritual growth should come from home. Many parents leave the responsibility totally up to their church. Your kids will model your attitudes and virtues towards God, more so than they will anyone else.

 **Idea File**

GIVE EACH CHILD TWO BOOK REPORT FORMS ALONG WITH TWO BOOKS AND TELL THEM THAT IF THEY FINISH THE BOOK AND FILL IN THE FORM THEY WILL RECEIVE A REWARD. BE SURE TO MAKE IT WORTH THEIR WHILE AND SEE HOW QUICKLY YOUR CHILDREN BECOME EXTRAORDINARY LEARNERS.

DESIGN A PERSONAL GROWTH SPOT FOR EACH OF YOUR CHILDREN

CREATE A SPECIAL CELEBRATION TO INTRODUCE YOUR CHILDREN TO THE CONCEPT OF PERSONAL GROWTH. GIVE THEM THEIR TOOLS IN A FORM OF A GIFT.

Book Report for Kids

Name: _____

Age: _____

Title of Book: _____

Author: _____

Began: _____   Finished:_____

Publisher:_____

What did I like most about this book?

What I can apply to my own life:

Ideas that came to me while reading:

Who could I recommend it to?

5 Raise a Reader

"If you want your children to grow above average, ensure that they develop solid reading skills."

-Stacia Pierce

Books ignite creativity, stir the imagination, illuminate curiosity and build a child's self-confidence. When children read it opens windows to the world that no one can close. If you foster daily reading habits in your children's early years the tradition of reading will soon become a part of their life's routine. Regardless of their ages, it's never too late to encourage the reading of books.

Older children may take a little more coercing to get them reading, but if you get creative I believe you will get them reading as well. Charles Tremendous Jones tells the story about his teenage son who he couldn't get to read. He came up with the idea to pay his son for every book he read, but it had to be his father's choice. His son agreed. Not long after their agreement began, his son became a lover of reading.

You can nurture your child's critical thinking skills by fostering his or her love of literature. When you expose your children to the right books it helps to shape their philosophy of life. Don't be reluctant in raising a reader. You have the ability to foster a desire for reading in each of your children. Incorporate a few of these easy to follow ideas and watch what happens!

10 Ways To Raise a Reader

1. MINGLE TOYS AND BOOKS

If you have an infant, it's never to early to introduce your baby to the world of books. If your child already has a toy box, add a few books to the pile of toys. Then the baby will associate books with play and fun.

2. SET UP A BOOK BASKET

For Ryan, I keep a big purple basket of books on the table in our sun room. So he has easy access to his books. My older daughter keeps most of her books on her bookshelf, but her new books that she's anxious to read she usually puts in her basket next to her bed.

3. TAKE YOUR KIDS BOOK SHOPPING

Encourage your children's interest in books by letting them help in the selection process. At lest twice a month I take the kids to the bookstore and let them choose a few new books. Sometimes we go to author appearances or book-signing events for children with one our children's favorite authors. Create a book fund to provide money for your kids to buy books of their own at least once per month. Owning your own books are a lot more exciting then having to return them to the library.

4. START A BOOK CLUB

Mother/son and mother/daughter book clubs are cropping up all over the US. These work best during the summer months when kids are out of school. Usually meeting twice a month to talk about the book and have some type of children's activity is sufficient. Not only will this help the mother - child bond, but it provides for a great social outlet.

5. VISIT CHILDREN'S BOOKSTORES

Today there are around three hundred children's bookstores across the United States. Boys and girls would love to visit such a store. The closest one to me is about a one hour drive to Grand Rapids, Michigan and it's called Pooh's Corner. My children love when we take a trip there. The store workers are so helpful in assisting the kids. Usually in a children's bookstore you can find very unique and hard to find books because it's their specialty.

6. READ TO YOUR CHILDREN

At some point your kids will grow out of this stage. But usually by that time reading will become a habit for them. Consider making bedtime stories a family affair. This is a good time to read Bible stories.

7. VISIT THE LIBRARY REGULARLY

Get your children their own library cards and take them to the library to pick out a few books. We usually visit the library in the summer time more than during the school year. Most schools also have their own library.

8. REWARD INDIVIDUAL READING.

I require my children to read something every day. I reward them for every five books that they read, with going out to dinner, or sometimes a clothing item. When it comes to encouraging your children to read consider a reward system.

9. CREATE A READING ENVIRONMENT

In most children's bookstores and at the library they have reading corners with colorful rugs, big bright colored pillows, beanbags, bright lights, and nearby shelves with an assortment of books. Kids are drawn to this environment, so why not do the same thing in your own home. Buy your kids their own bookshelves and create a colorful bright place that's cozy enough for them to want to sit and read.

10. BUILD A BASIC BOOK COLLECTION

Allow each child to have his or her very own book collection. Many children books come in series. If your child is drawn to a particular line of books, help them build a collection of the series.

Dictionaries, Bibles, encyclopedias, almanacs are all good reference materials that should be a part of every child's collection. Special interest - What are you children interested in? What do they dream of becoming? You might want to help them build a collection of special interest books that relate to their hobbies, curiosities and dreams. For example, my daughter Ariana has a collection of books on cheerleading and entrepreneurship for kids. Whatever you choose from the selections I outlined, you are sure to enrich the life of your children if you get them interested in reading books.

Reading Enhancers:

📖 Show youngsters how to look at the table of contents and index of a book to see what kind of information is inside.

📖 Buy your kids their own book plates so they can put their name and purchase date on each book.

📖 Display book posters. My daughter has a really nice one in her room that I had custom framed to match her room colors.

📖 Use books to plan vacations. We made a trip to Washington, D.C. after our children read about the White House and Lincoln Memorial. We vacationed in Philadelphia after reading about Betty Ross and the first flag and the Liberty Bell.

📖 Make a book report form during the summer months. Have your kids do a simple book report on each book they read then review them.

📖 Keep a chart of how many books each child reads per year. Show them their progress.

📖 Monitor what your kids are reading, especially your youth. The older your kids are the more monitoring you will have to do, but kids should not have free reign to choose just any type of books they want. Today, even in school, there's many suggestions for teenagers to read books that promote fornication, drinking, drugs and way ward lifestyles.

At least three times a week I read
bedtime stories to my children. They
look so forward to this special time
of interaction. Extensive research
has proven that reading aloud to a
child is the single most important
factor in raising a reader.

Yet with the hectic schedules of most moms today, the idea of
sitting still for thirty minutes to read a book rather than a TV show
seems overwhelming. But take a look at your schedule again;
believe it or not, incorporating reading time is possible.

You want to cultivate a desire for reading in your children by
showing them rather than telling them the value of reading. It's
simple to show value buy books, and take trips to the library on
a regular basis. Spend time reading yourself. Have a book filled
home. Here's some other ideas that have worked with my
children. Introduce them to a character they love. My son Ryan
is hooked on *Veggie Tales*[1] and he can relate to the characters in
their books.

My daughter Ariana likes the *Baby Sitter's Club*, *Mary Kate
and Ashley* and *Clueless*.[2] She has almost every book in the
series. What's your children's interest? There's bound to be a
book about it. When Ariana first showed an interest in cheerleading
I found some great children's books about cheerleaders. Then
the year she decided to start her own business I bought her
several books for children on how to start a business. When
children read about something they love, it will stir their creativity
and expand their outlook.

Building a collection of books around a child's interest can also help direct them for their future careers. When I was a child I had a great interest in books about fashion, modeling, self-esteem, beauty and image. My mother helped me build a collection of books on these subjects. Once I became an adult, my collection served me as a great library of resources to aid me in my career. My daughter Ariana has a collection of books on tea parties. She loves hosting tea parties, so every book I see about tea parties for children I buy her.

Ariana, also seems to be interested in self help books so I have helped her build an outstanding collection of self-help and self-improvement should she decide to be a motivational speaker herself. I can tell by her compassion for helping people that her mission will definitely be to bring positive change in the lives of others. Reading is a productive way to spend time. When you raise your children to be readers of good books, you can raise a child who welcomes self-development. A child who will eventually study and learn on their own . In Karen O'Connors book, *How to Hook Your Kids on Books* (Nelson), she asserts that books strengthen, inspire, motivate and encourage healthy self-esteem and foster understanding, affection and respect for others. I agree books are a powerful mechanism to steer your kids in a positive direction.

 **Idea File**

📖 GO BOOK SHOPPING WITH YOUR KIDS. SPEND AS MUCH TIME AS THEY DESIRE. ENCOURAGE THEM TO FIND AT LEAST ONE BOOK TO BUY. EVEN IF YOUR CHILD SEEMS A LITTLE RESISTANT AT FIRST. IF YOU PROMISE TO GIVE A REWARD TO THEM FOR FINISHING THE BOOK, YOU'LL IMMEDIATELY SEE THEIR ATTITUDE CHANGE.

📖 LOOK AROUND YOUR HOUSE. HOW MANY BOOKS DO YOUR KIDS OWN? WHAT KINDS OF BOOKS ARE THEY?

📖 WHAT ARE YOUR KIDS READING? THIS WILL GIVE YOU A CLUE TO HOW MUCH TIME YOU MAY NEED TO COMMIT TO THIS AREA IN YOU CHILDREN'S LIFE.

6 Raise a Writer

"Winners always write down how they won."

- Stacia Pierce

No matter what your kids' future goals are, writing is an essential skill for success in life. Writing fosters reading just as reading motivates writing. Children who write are generally children who read. Since I am an author I probably do a little more than the average person might do to foster writing in my children, but I know that good writing skills will help your kids make good grades in school as well as in life.

I was pleased to learn from Ariana's teacher that in school she is very particular about her writing assignments and takes her time to print her words neatly. This means she's giving attention to details. What an excellent quality to possess at such a young age. My son Ryan loves sitting in his high chair with paper and crayons and drawing his art creations. As soon as he could hold a crayon I bought him writing tools, to introduce him to the wonderful world of writing.

Good writing skills is an essential ingredient for achievement. Studies has shown that more than three fourths of those entering the nations workforce between now and 2000 will have limited verbal and writing skills. These startling statistics spill over to our youth. Studies have shown the most influential variable in a child's participation and success in school is the parental educational level. That means as parents we must take responsibility for our child's education.

Good writers become good thinkers and more motivated learners. They will earn higher grades in school. Kids who write at home do much better on writing assignments given from school. By fostering several opportunities for writing at home you open your child up to many benefits. They will use writing to build friendships, become excellent note takers, and learn to write down important information which could help in taking class notes. Sometimes kids don't excel in school because they have poor writing skills.

8 Ways To Raise A Writer

1. Give Your Kids A Journal

A journal is an excellent way to introduce children to writing. It is a private book especially for them. At first you will probably have to coax your kids into making regular entries. But after a while they'll like the private time and will look forward to recording their thoughts and ideas. I have purchased several journals for my daughter. *All About Me* by Linda Kranz[1] is a keepsake journal for kids with thought starters on each page. It's an excellent starter journal for kids ages 8-15 years old.

My Faith Journal by Karen Hill has two versions. One for boys and one for girls. This Christian journal is excellent. It's filled with colorful illustrations and lots of scripture references and has character building thought starters. I have given away several of these journals to my nieces and my nephews and my daughters friends as birthday gifts.

Every child I gave one to declares it is the best journal they ever had. To help trigger creativity in Ariana's journalizing I bought her all the editions of *Amelia's Notebook,* by Marissa Moss[3]. These inspirational books are like reading someone's personal journal. Amelia's Notebooks are full of creative ideas like pasting letters you receive to a journal page, drawing how you feel, pasting theater tickets of a movie you loved and much more. Sometimes kids need visuals of what to do to get them started.

2. BUY A TRAVEL JOURNAL

Whenever you take a short trip or a long vacation, encourage your kids to write about their experience. Travel journals are great because you couple photographs with words to relive your experience. I have a nice collection of stickers my kids can add to decorate their travel journals.

3. ENCOURAGE LETTER WRITING

Introduce your kids to writing by providing the supplies and space they need to experiment with it. Buy your kids their own stationary, pens and colored pencils. Then help them decorate the container where their supplies will go in so it's user friendly. Buy them a desk chair and a writing lamp for their bedroom or set up an art station in a playroom or in the basement. Another good idea is to start a family tradition where once a month your kids write a letter to another family member or friend. To stimulate children's writing enthusiasm, buy them books about letter writing. There's a good book on letter writing for girls called *Clever Letters* by American Girl.[4]

4. INTRODUCE YOUR KIDS TO A BOOK DIARY

Put together a book diary by purchasing a 3 ring binder with a clear pocket. Have your kids create a cover to slip inside the pocket. Then create book report forms. I'm creating a book diary for my kids. There will be a boy and girl version out this summer. The book reports are an excellent way to record and remember important facts, ideas, quotes, and information about the book.

5. ENCOURAGE YOUR CHILD TO WRITE A BOOK

My daughter made and wrote her first book at the age of six. We bought a *Make Your Own Book Kit* from the bookstore. We had to actually make the glue to bind the book and pages together. It was a hard cover book. Ariana had to design the cover and write her own story on the inside pages. She came up with the idea of pasting a photo of herself on the cover and entitled it *"All About Ariana"*.

6. GIVE YOUR CHILD A WRITER'S NOTEBOOK

A writer's notebook is just simply a lined notebook that an individual child would be attracted to. Keeping a writer's notebook can help kids become more alive to the world. The purpose of the notebook is to gather interesting newsworthy data. It can help them develop the habit of paying attention to little pictures and images in the world that they might otherwise ignore. Teenage children will especially benefit from a writer's notebook. This is where they can collect and record ideas for book reports, stories they want to write in the school newspaper, poems, plays or even possible use for their own publications.

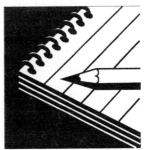

I read an article in the **_Grand Rapids Press_** (July 4, 1998) about a fifteen year old teen author who got a six figure deal from Zondervan for a fifty state book. Amy Burritt self-published a book in May called _My American Adventure._[6] It's about meeting 44 of the 50 governors of the United States as her family traveled by motor home across the country. She recorded all her information while on their vacation in journals or a writer's notebook, which formed the basis of her book that Zondervan bought out from her. Kids can accomplish extraordinary things when provided with the proper tools, atmosphere and information.

7. GET AGE APPROPRIATE MAGAZINE SUBSCRIPTIONS

Subscribing your kids to children's and teen magazines will expose your kids to great writing. For girls ages 7-14 I personally think _American Girl_ magazine is the best. _BRIO_[7] is also a nice Christian magazine for teen girls. _Sports Illustrated Kids_[8] is excellent for boys. Look through magazines before making a choice because many magazines on the market today don't promote good values.

8. Pen Pals

Having a pen pal encourages on-going writing. **"Through a lively correspondence with a pen pal your child gains insight into how people live in other cultures", says Cheri Fuller.** You can have your kids become pen pals with one of their relatives who lives in another state. It's a great way for kids to keep in touch with each other as well.

Treat your children's writing with respect. This will help them develop a good self image and a willingness to keep writing.

 Idea File

🖊 Take your kids on a writer's shopping trip to buy journals, pens and markers.

🖊 Have your children keep a "summer adventure" journal to help them develop their writing skills.

🖊 Fill a rolling cart with art and writing supplies.

7 Raise an Achiever

"An achiever always visualizes what can be done in the future."

- Stacia Pierce

As a parent you have to provide your kids with the proper atmosphere, tools, books, and information to help them achieve. The world we live in today is so different from former generations. Today we have to raise our kids to be global minded at a young age. We have to expose them to the computer, the Internet and even get them to take foreign languages like Spanish or Chinese. In the future people will work more from home, running home based businesses; and link themselves to the world by modern technology. Our kids will need to develop their skills to be high achievers in our world today.

The kids who will achieve will be self-sufficient and independent. An achiever is one who purposefully reaches for and attains his goals. Your kids won't move in the direction of being a high achiever without your assistance. God wants our children to be achievers, and He will become their learning partner. James 1:5 says: "If any of you lack wisdom let him ask of God." When you teach your kids how to hook up with God through prayer and asking for help, you will provide them with the foundation they need to be achievers. Next, take some practical steps to guide them into becoming achievers.

13 Ways to Help Your Kids Achieve

1. ENCOURAGE THEM TO TRY NEW THINGS AND INVITE THE UNEXPECTED. The first time I took my kids to the art lounge, they were so excited about decorating and painting their very own dishes. Before our trip they didn't realize that they could design their own creations.

2. INVOLVE THEM IN AFTER SCHOOL ACTIVITIES. School can be so grade oriented that other talents go unrecognized. Make sure your child gets the opportunity to test their creative genius, whether it's taking music lessons, an art class, cheerleading or playing sports.

3. VISIT MUSEUMS AND HISTORICAL SITES. Almost all kids love the "hands on" fun of children's museums. Museums offer a safe environment in which children can explore, learn and ask questions. On every vacation we take, usually we add to our "to do list" a visit to the museum.

4. INTRODUCE YOUR KIDS TO ART. Present an art gallery as a recreational event rather than an educational one. It's a chance to explore some place new, and look at what's interesting. Top off the trip with a visit to the ice cream shop or bakery. Your kids will remember the experience as fun and not boring.

5. COMPILE A SCRAPBOOK OF YOUR CHILD'S ACHIEVE-
MENTS AWARDS AND PROGRESS. Display it where guests can
pick it up and browse through it. This shows them that you are
proud of them.

6. BUY A COMPUTER FOR YOUR
HOME. Today computers expand the
boundaries of what kids can accomplish.
Whether it's reading stories in their own
voices, designing cards and banners, composing
music, painting a picture, making tatoos, doll clothes and nail
stickers, or creating reports for school with computer graphics,
maps or graphs- a home computer will give your child an edge.
You will put your child at a great disadvantage if you do not own
a computer. If you have only one computer but several children,
make a schedule so that everyone can share.

7. ENCOURAGE YOUR CHILDREN TO EXPRESS THEIR OPINIONS
DURING FAMILY CONVERSATIONS.
The old expression, "kids should be seen and not heard," is a very
shallow philosophy. To raise kids who are achievers they must feel
like their parents value what they have to say whether they agree
totally with them or not. Create situations that let your children have
a direct influence. Involve them in home repairs, cooking, and things
that show their efforts get results.

8. ENROLL YOUR CHILDREN IN A FOREIGN LANGUAGE.
Learning a second language will be essential for your kids' future,
especially if they ever do international business. In many schools,

foreign language courses aren't available until high school which is well past the time when children are most likely to embrace a second language as their own, so don't wait. Find an after-school course or buy a software package and let them learn on their computer at home.

9. REMEMBER THE POWER OF PRAISE

Avoid criticism at all cost. The most powerful motivating force available to a parent is praise. It can be done in a variety of ways. You can send a card to congratulate outstanding behavior or you might give your children certificates of achievement for good performances. Catch them doing something right and respond to it.

10. BELIEVE YOUR CHILDREN CAN ACHIEVE GREAT THINGS.

Did you know most humans only use eight percent of their mental capacity? That means people are capable of so much more. Sometimes kids limit themselves because they don't believe they can accomplish great things. When given the right opportunities and encouragement, children can accomplish incredible things. I tell my kids constantly, "You can achieve great things" and "God has ordained you for greatness."

11. RAISE A PROBLEM SOLVER

When your child gets stuck on a book report or has difficulty with a science project it's natural to want to rescue them. But learning to overcome problems is essential to a child's success. Over-protectiveness can make a child think that they are not as capable as other people. Allow them to make a few mistakes, it's all a part of the learning process. You could help them by asking probing questions like, "What don't you understand? What solutions can you come up with?" etc.

12. LET YOUR CHILDREN SEE YOU WORK

Share your interest in cooking, gardening, volunteering, or writing, The most important thing you can give your children is a passion for something. My children see me go through the process of writing my books, which allows them to see how much commitment it takes before getting to the end result. Don't always send your kids outside to play while you cook; instead have them assist you. Children of employed and nonemployed mother's develop equally well, so if you work, don't feel guilty. Simply decide to make the most of your time with your kids.

13. TALK TO YOUR CHILDREN

Talk a lot, even to your newborn. Let your child know you are available and accessible to listen. Don't always cut them off when they ask questions or begin talking; stop and listen. Over the Christmas holiday Ariana's grandparents on my husband's side spent a few days with us. What a rewarding time to pull on their years of wisdom. Ariana was full of excitement and began asking her grandma one question after the other. I said, "Ariana, give her a rest", and my mother in law responded with, "Ariana will be such a bright child because she is not afraid of learning. She asks so many wise questions." What an enlightenment; that's another way to look at it. I thought to myself, "I better make sure I'm not hindering her from talking and learning and growing into an achiever."

 **Idea File**

🏆 WHAT STRATEGIES ARE YOU CURRENTLY USING TO HELP YOUR CHILDREN BECOME ACHIEVERS? WRITE OUT FOUR NEW STRATEGIES YOU'LL USE WITHIN THE NEXT SIXTY DAYS TO HELP YOUR CHILDREN DEVELOP INTO LIFELONG ACHIEVERS.

1.
2.
3.
4.

8 Raise a Leader

"Today a reader, tomorrow a leader."

- W. Fusselman

I believe any child can become a leader. Although some children come to it more easily than others, probably based upon their inherent personality types, all have potential which can be developed with practice and training.

Last year my husband trained my daughter how to stand before an audience and introduce herself. At the first few practices, she had her head down and fidgeted, but after several sessions, Ariana readily walked up to the podium, confidently introduced herself, and went on to communicate with her audience.

From that experience I knew that children can learn to be leaders. Leadership skills include self-confidence, friendliness, persuasiveness and helpfulness.

At a recent parent/teacher conference Ariana's teacher shared with me that Ariana was a real leader in her class. When she gets done with her work first she will go help many of the other students. Real leaders will assist others but not bully them.

7 Ways To Raise A Leader

Remember to give your kids leadership opportunities working with people in the church youth group, or organizing a neighborhood summer block party. When you encourage these types of leadership roles you give your child a chance to bloom.

1. ENCOURAGE COMMUNICATION SKILLS

Part of being a leader is possessing the ability to persuade. To be persuasive you have to communicate well. Ariana's Dad was teaching her communication skills when he had her practice introducing herself. Also engage in meaningful conversations with your children. Surround your children with good books, and dictionaries. Have them read aloud.

2. INTRODUCE THE IDEA OF LEADERSHIP

Draw attention to other leaders. Buy your children inspiring biographies of other young adults who have done something admirable. Openly talk to your children about being a leader and tell them it's good to positively influence others.

3. BE A ROLE MODEL

Your children are bound to imitate the behavior you demonstrate. Take a leadership role by heading up a project at your children's school or by mentoring another mother who has a little less experience than you. Share with your children how your leadership is benefiting others.

4. ALLOW THEM OPPORTUNITIES TO MAKE DECISIONS

Leadership is knowing how to make choices on your own. We decided that when our children reached a certain age, we would let them help in decorating their room. Ask your children what colors they want to be surrounded with. Ariana also helps plan family vacations. She helps make decisions on what sights we'll visit and where we will eat.

5. ENCOURAGE LEADERSHIP ACTIVITIES

During the summer we encourage entrepreneurship by having Ariana decide on a business she will start and run. There's several leadership skills involved in entrepreneurship: imagination - to know what people need; creativity-to come up with an idea and fill a need; energy - to do the work; determination -to finish what you start and courage- to believe in yourself.

6. GIVE RECOGNITION TO ANY LEADERSHIP EFFORTS

When you notice your child stepping forward to take a leadership role, offer encouragement by telling them you're proud of them daring to step out. Give ribbons, plaques, certificates and trophies of your own to reward leadership efforts. The exciting news is that all these skills can be taught to your children. And you can raise a self-confident leader.

7. Expose Your Child to Many Vocations

Let him spend a day observing a business executive, doctor or lawyer or even let him do volunteer work for a few weeks if they are old enough. Allow them the opportunity to watch problem solvers in action. Problem solving is a key ingredient in all leaders. So step back and let your kids explore.

 **Idea File**

! Give each of your children the opportunity to practice leadership skills this week. Identify to the child just how they practiced leadership; then commend them for it.

For example: Pick a night to have dinner as a family. Then allow the children to choose topics for discussion.

Teach Money Matters

CATHY WRAY

"We do our kids an injustice when we don't teach them about money."

-Author Unknown

Teaching kids about money and money management should always begin with teaching them to give. Studies show that the most productive and prosperous individuals in America are people who contribute generously to some sort of charity, church or other worthy cause. According to *Fortune Magazine*, 40 of Americas wealthiest people are the most generous givers, contributing an estimated 11% of their net profits to private foundations, charitable organizations, schools and communities.[1]

Extraordinary means just that - out of the ordinary! Out of the ordinary people have learned the law of giving. The Bible says that if we will acknowledge God in all of our ways, He will direct our paths. I believe our giving should first begin with God.

Tithes & Offerings

Our youngest daughter Jasmine is by far the biggest giver of our three children. Jasmine will usually give an offering that matches her tithes, no matter how much money she receives. For her birthday, Jasmine received a little more than $100 in cash from relatives. The following church service she gave in tithes and offerings a total of $50 The $50 she had left was not enough to purchase the outfits she had earmarked in her *Delia* catalogue, so she prayed and believed God for her increase. Not even a week after she sowed her seed, her grandmother called and invited her to a week-long, all expense paid (including airfare and shopping) vacation! Grandmothers are a lot like God; They always do exceeding, abundantly more than you can imagine. At the age of thirteen, Jasmine has the testimony of getting almost everything she asks for, all the time. I believe it's because she has learned to honor God first, and is not afraid to give generously. When you teach your children to plant generous seeds, they can expect to receive an abundant harvest.

Savings Accounts & Investments

A recent article in *Parents* Magazine revealed that the number one thing teens wished their families would talk more about is family finances. In fact, nearly 4 in 10 youth surveyed said they  would like to understand more about family budgeting, saving and investing. (Jan. 1998) Statistics show that teens rake in about $102 billion from jobs, allowances, gifts and other sources. Of that $102 billion they will spend approximately $67 billion on cd's, clothes, movies, food and other extravagances.[2]

As a parent, you can help your young person develop the skills necessary to manage money wisely. Of course, saving every penny is not necessary, but deliberately planning what amount will go into savings will increase long-term financial stability for teens.

Most teenagers don't have regular monthly bills to pay yet, but ALL teenagers have a good idea what purchases they want to make as soon as they have a little extra cash. Surprisingly, many young people are actually concerned about their future. They want to be prepared. Encouraging your young person to create a spending plan now will help them manage financial responsibility for the rest of their life.

The key to success with finances is budgeting; a systematic method of tracking income and expenditures. The average teen handles their finances in much the same way as they have seen their parents handle the family finances. Whatever things were important in your household will probably be important to your children as they grow up. Your child should be thoroughly instructed on finances in at least five categories: earning, giving, saving, spending, and borrowing. Many adults have become financial failures because they made "wants" into "needs". Their priorities were things that had nothing to do with building financial success. According to the *Wall Street Journal* seventy percent of all Americans have no money left over from their paycheck after basic expenses each month (NCFE News Release 1998).

When spending is planned and priorities are set, it helps us separate the wants from the real needs. A savings account is a must for every person. The sooner you start your children saving, the more stable their future will be. If your child began saving as young as 12 years old - only $1 a day -- they would be a millionaire by the age of 45!

Savings accounts are very easy to open. Most any financial institution will open one with a minimum deposit of $5. If your children receive regular income from allowances or earnings, you should have them designate a specific amount that goes into a savings every time they get paid. Saving a mere 5% of your total income will usually make a pretty good nest egg. Keep in mind though, it's not the dollar amount that's important; it's developing the habit of wise money management.

Each one of our children have savings accounts in their own name. They are required to deposit a certain percentage of any income they receive into their account. In addition to their deposits, we have a regular amount direct deposited into their accounts right from our pay checks. Savings should not be used for casual spending. It should only be considered for major, planned expenditures, or for emergencies. Maintaining a savings account will take discipline, but it is essential for future financial success. God will bless us with increase when we've shown discipline with what we have. If your teen can identify a savings objective, like perhaps $500 by summer's end or enough money for a football uniform, then it's much easier for them to save. It also builds self-confidence each time a financial goal is met.

Once you open a savings account for your child, you will need to teach them how to keep track of their money. Sometimes financial institutions make mistakes! In order to be good stewards over what God has given us we must watch over our income and put it to good use.

Take the time to teach your child how to track their expenditures. Carefully review the monthly statements, comparing them to the personal register. If they are able to make ATM transactions, be sure to include them when you're reconciling your accounts.

Young children give parents the best opportunity to encourage good financial habits. As soon as your child is able to add and subtract, use a simple budget like the one provided in this chapter (Exhibit 1) to help them understand the concept of income and expenses.

Have your child add up all their sources for income for the week. Throughout the week have them enter what they spend in the "Actual" spending column. At the end of the first week, help your child total the expenses and subtract them from the income. If spending exceeds income, put a check mark in the "over" column; if it is less, check the "under" column. Depending on the final results for the week, you can teach your child ways to increase their income or reduce expenditures.

71

PERSONAL BUDGET (Exhibit 1)

Day	Income	Planned	Actual	Total	Under	Over
		Spending		Total	Goal	
Mon.					☐	☐
Tue.					☐	☐
Wed					☐	☐
Thur					☐	☐
Fri					☐	☐
Sat					☐	☐
Sun					☐	☐

It is important for parents to show children the "big picture when it comes to handling finances. Make the financial world accessible and tangible to your child. Young people should become familiar with the financial sections of the local newspaper, the library, and the Internet. Encourage them to do exercises and activities that will develop their financial prowess, like creating an imaginary "stock portfolio" of companies that make products they like. Track the investment results with them; you might learn something too!

The most important step to preparing your child for the future is helping them get a vision for where they want to end up in life. Your child can be light years ahead of their peers by simply determining now what they want their life to be like.

 **Idea File**

💰 GIVE YOUR CHILD RESPONSIBILITIES: CREATE OPPORTUNITIES FOR THEM TO EARN MONEY

💰 HELP YOUR CHILD PLAN AND SAVE FOR THE THINGS THEY WANT.

💰 GIVE YOUR CHILD GUIDELINES FOR WHAT YOU EXPECT HIM/HER TO SAVE FROM THEIR EARNINGS.

💰 INVOLVE YOUR CHILD IN THE FAMILY'S FINANCIAL DECISION-MAKING.

💰 GIVE YOUR CHILD A PIGGY BANK OR OPEN A SAVINGS ACCOUNT FOR THEM AT THE BANK, SO THEY HAVE A PLACE TO PUT THEIR EARNED INCOME.

Organize Your Kids

CATHY WRAY

"It is wonderful how much may be done if we are always doing."

-Thomas Jefferson

We adults have learned over time that life seems so much simpler when there are systems in place to keep us on track. That's why when we enter the work force, we are given job descriptions. Job descriptions are simply a type of system that helps us know what we're supposed to be doing, and help our employer know if, in fact, we're doing it.

Create a Chores List

I think of a chores list as a mini job description. It briefly outlines the exact details that are expected of each family member. Our kids have occasional bouts of selective amnesia, so the chores list we've developed has a task guide with little boxes for them to initial when they have completed each task. For instance, if Jasmine has kitchen duty, some of the tasks for her duty might be: a) Have I wiped the counter and stove clean? Yes or no: or b) Have I put away all the dishes? Yes or no; Following the task guide helps her do her job completely and reminds her of what we expect of her. When allowance time (payday) rolls around, we use that same task guide to determine if each person had met the goals we've established for getting the chores done.

Make a Household Notebook

Most things seem to run a lot better if there is one central place for important information. There's a certain security in knowing where to find the information you need. We created a household notebook to house all of the pertinent reference information that any one of us might need. A household notebook doesn't have to be anything elaborate. I use an 8 1/2 x 11 looseleaf binder that has colored tabbed dividers to separate sections for school calendars, work schedules and the chores list so everyone knows what they are supposed to do and when they are supposed to do it. I also have a section with emergency telephone numbers and contact persons and a checklist for my kid's care givers when I'm away. The checklist lets whoever is in charge know when bedtime is, when television time is over, what we normally allow our kids to eat, how long they can talk on the phone and anything else that's important for sticking to our established regiment.

Organizing a Blended Family

Nowadays there are plenty of situations where integrating each child in an equitable way may seem a bit difficult initially. When a child comes to live with you, there may be some apprehension about setting rules or very little knowledge about the child's previous upbringing. Notwithstanding, the child will probably have already established certain habits that are contrary to your family's lifestyle. Our oldest daughter, Nikki came to live with us two years ago. She is not biologically related to me or my husband, so it would have been very easy to make things a little easier for

76

Nikki in the name of making her transition smooth. Unfortunately, if we had done this our other kids would have resented her and us, and Nikki would have never really been a true part of our family. When it was certain that Nikki would be with us long term, we immediately included her on the chores list. We made her accountable to our house rules just like the others. There was no special treatment to help her fit in; in fact, the best way to help her fit in was to treat her like she was already "in."

Parents need to take responsibility for how the home runs. We set the tone for the home. Anyone who lives in your home is under your authority and is subject to your house rules. When Nikki came to live with us, our routines and expectations were already established. She didn't have the same points of reference that we  had on everything, but because we were consistent with our expectations, Nikki conformed. Every parent has the God-given ability to bring kids, step-kids, live-ins or whatever other situations there might be, into your structure and your way of life.

Today, it's hard for someone who doesn't know us to have an inkling that she is not ours. We refer to her as our daughter and we're involved in her life as much as with our other children. We can tell that we've made a positive impact in Nikki's life, and the standards of how we run our home didn't have to change.

Have Family Meetings

Statistics indicate that the number one reason for divorce is lack of communication. While it is still somewhat uncommon for parents and children to get divorced, we often alienate our kids because we don't allow an opportunity for them to be heard. For any organization to run effectively, each part of the organization must feel that they are a valued part and that their opinion matters. Every dictatorship in the span of time has suffered revolt.

In our regular family meetings we give our kids an opportunity to express their feelings about how our home is run and offer suggestions for improvement and modification. Let me caution you - in order for this type of format to work properly, you must establish ground rules. Our kids can voice a complaint, but they must always address us appropriately and respectfully.

If they have a problem, they must offer a viable solution to the problem. Having family meetings have taught us some things too. Our kids were a lot smarter than we gave them credit for, and we didn't always have the right answers just because we were the parents. They actually came up with some very good ideas that helped our family run better.

You can hold family meetings to discuss upcoming events, vacations, birthdays, complaints or other issues that may come up.

Help Your Kids Plan Their Day

It's has already been established that most kids do pretty much what they see their parents do, especially in the home. So, if you're just now deciding that your family and your home needs some organization after years of clutter and chaos, then it will take a bit of planning to get everyone involved.

Start by taking a few moments to plan each day. Do this in the morning or at night , whichever is more convenient. Get your kids involved by going over the master to-do list with them. Check out your calendar for upcoming events and appointments, then go over their school calendars and sports events or other activities. Don't forget to schedule time for reading, prayer, and study. Once you've written down everything that must be done, you and your kids can prioritize each task. If your family schedules allow it, try to have your children follow the same routine each day. Once being organized becomes a habit, it will be difficult to break.

Establish Daily Routines

Routines are simply repetitious actions. They get us in the "habit" of doing the same thing, the same way, every time. Decide what time everyone needs to be up in the morning; then divy up bathroom times. Give everyone an alarm clock so each child is responsible for waking themselves up. We made the mistake of being the human alarm clocks far too long. Have your kids do as much as possible the night before, so they don't feel rushed in the morning. Make each family member responsible for noting their time commitments on the calendar.

Create Designated Areas

The key to being organized is having everything in its proper place. Not only can we put things in there proper place, we can create areas that are appropriate for specific tasks. To give you a picture of what I mean, in our home we have some designated areas. The office is used for homework, study, and research. The office houses the computer, typewriter, fax, file folders, encyclopedias and almost everything anyone would need to complete an office or school task. The recreation area has the ping-pong table the video games, and other play things. Consequently, when we go into those areas, our mind set automatically adjusts to fit the environment.

As parents, we have to be careful that we're not promoting some forms of disorganization in our children. Our kids get unconsciously confused because they're trying to study in the recreation room or trying to play in the study room.

Create designated areas in your home that are realistic and work. Have the right equipment for the designated task in each area. You'll be amazed how a small thing like changing the atmosphere can lead to a more organized lifestyle.

 **Idea File**

☺ CREATE A CHORES LIST SO EVERYONE KNOWS WHAT IS EXPECTED OF THEM.

☺ MAKE EACH CHILD FEEL LIKE A VALUED PART OF THE FAMILY.

☺ MAKE A HOUSEHOLD NOTEBOOK. IT'S AN EXCELLENT RE-SOURCE FOR BABY-SITTERS, HOUSEKEEPERS, OR OVERNIGHT GUESTS.

☺ HAVE FAMILY MEETINGS ON A REGULAR BASIS.

☺ ESTABLISH DAILY ROUTINES. DAILY AGENDAS HELP EVERYONE BECOME ROUTINE ORIENTED.

☺ CREATE DESIGNATED AREAS FOR STUDY, PRAYER , GAMES, ETC.

☺ HELP YOUR KIDS PLAN THEIR DAY. THIS IS A GREAT OPPORTU-NITY FOR QUALITY TIME WITH THEM WHILE INSTILLING ORGANIZA-TIONAL HABITS.

☺ BALANCE FUN AND WORK. SCHEDULE IN FUN TIME.

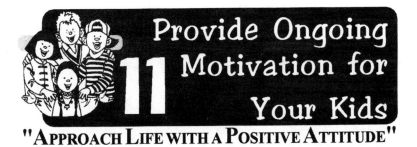

Provide Ongoing Motivation for Your Kids

"APPROACH LIFE WITH A POSITIVE ATTITUDE"

"Nothing great was ever achieved without enthusiasm."
- John A. Shedd

To raise extraordinary kids you must understand that to provide ongoing motivation for yourself and the kids is essential. Motivation means to be moved to action, to provide with an incentive or motive. So when I talk about motivating your kids, I'm talking about getting them to be moved to take action. Giving them an optimistic view point of life itself.

Researchers at the Search Institute, a nonprofit research organization surveyed nearly 100,000 sixth and twelfth graders on whether or not they posses certain developmental assets and how these assets affected their life. These assets included things such as involvement in church and school, family support and optimism about the future. The results? The more positive assets a child has, the more likely he is to grow up competent, caring and the less likely he is to engage in risky activities such as drug abuse and violence.[1.]

Today kids are surrounded by negativity from the news and even at school, so to live in a positive environment at home gives them hope for a bright future.

83

8 Ways To Provide Ongoing Motivation

1. SEND LUNCH BOX NOTES

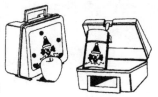

At least once a week I try to put a inspirational note into my children's lunch box. This simple idea reminds your child how much you care. Plus the encouraging words you write will totally lift their spirits. Recently I purchased a booklet called, *Lots of Love in a Lunch Box* by Joy L. Stevens[2] from the Christian book store. This book is filled with 75 colorful tear out notes to brighten your child's day. The pre-made notes make brightening my children's day so easy and convenient.

2. MAIL A MOTIVATIONAL CARD

While card shopping to replenish my stock, about a year ago, I discovered a line of cards by Hallmark for kids. They had motivational message and space left for you to fill in your own thoughts. I bought every one I could find. I usually mail them to my  own kids when I'm away on a trip, or I send them one of those cards with a gift when they do something exceptional.

3. REWARD SUCCESS

Ariana put on her dream list last year that she wanted to be a straight "A" student. Throughout the year I reminded Ariana of her dreams and goals and offered my support to help her accomplish her dreams. Just this week I went to parent/teacher conferences and discovered that she's a straight "A" student. As a matter of fact she had many A pluses. Her father rewarded her with five dollars for every A. She had a total of twelve, six from her classes and six for conduct and behavior. She was rewarded $60.00 and immediately began to plan how she could achieve the same results next marking period. Reward your children for a job well done. Children are motivated to work hard when they know there is a reward for their efforts.

4. PROVIDE MOTIVATIONAL TAPES

My husband is one of the most exciting teachers of the Word I have ever heard. The youth and children in our church love to listen to their Pastor minister the word. We often encourage our children to listen to the teaching tapes or lessons taught on a regular basis by their pastors. I also provide motivational tapes geared toward children for my kids to listen to. My favorite children's motivational tapes are by Bob Moaward. Bob used to be a school teacher, but now he is a consultant and motivational speaker. His tape series include: "You Got What It Takes," and "You're Natures Greatest Miracle" for children ages six to fourteen. Bob also has *Wordcraft*, an advanced vocabulary builder for kids and *Unlocking your Potential* for youth ages fourteen through seventeen years old. I'm very careful about what type of motivational materials I expose myself or my children to, because most of the secular materials have views and values that are contrary to my own. The best motivational tapes you can listen to are from seasoned inspiring Pastors and Christian teachers or leaders.

5. PRACTICE AN EXCITING AFTER-SCHOOL RITUAL.

Welcome your kids home in a positive manner. Ask exciting questions like: "What happened at school that was fun? What exciting new things did you learn?" Then once they settle down ask them, "Did anything go on at school today that you would like to discuss?" This will send a positive message to your kids about school.

Have peaceful music playing while you're waiting for your kids to arrive home from school. Have the kitchen table set with simple bright colored napkins, paper plates and a healthy snack. This sends a motivational message to my daughter  that I'm excited about her return home. Oftentimes teenagers have after-school activities, so they come home later. What a welcome home ritual does is it keeps your children from getting involved in other after-school activities simply because they hate coming home.

6. BUY BOOKS THAT ARE POSITIVE.

Provide your kids with books that stir their creativity and open their minds to new thoughts and ideas, that will move them to action. Last Christmas I bought Ariana a book called *The World of William Joyce Scrapbook*.[4] The book describes how the authors write a book from beginning to end. This book was so inspiring that I have read it several times myself. After my daughter read the book she began to draw more in her journal and she took her writing very seriously.

7. Make Reading the Bible a Family Value.

The Bible is the most motivational book your kids could ever read. I want to build a strong family heritage with my kids of reading the Bible and praying. I purchased an empty basket for Ariana last Christmas and called it her prayer basket. I filled it with her very own children's study Bible, highlighter, a prayer journal and a devotional. Her Bible is set up to read a section every day, and then she will have completed the Bible in one year.

I encourage her to read her Bible every night before going to bed. Now both Ariana and Ryan are being exposed to hearing the Bible on tape. My dad just recently gave my children the entire King James version of the Bible on cassette. Lately every night when Ariana gets in bed she turns the tape on and it plays until it stops. Usually she falls asleep before it ends, but the Word still gets in her spirit.

8. Brighten the Day with Motivational Words

Use bright, colorful and cheerful words when communicating especially with your children. When Ryan learns a new word or follows directions given to him, everyone in the household knows to say, "Ryan, that's great" and clap excitedly for him. You should see how it motivates him. Whenever people applaud him, his eyes light up, a big smile shines on his face, and oftentimes, he'll run in a circle and clap for himself. Even babies need praise and motivation. Every single day my husband and I tell our kids; "we love you" and give them lots of hugs. "I love you" are words of security. Scientists have proven that when babies don't get enough touching and holding, they don't develop properly. You

87

should send signals of love both verbally and physically on a daily basis. Encourage positive self-talk. Correct your kids when your hear them making a belittling statement about themselves. Most of all, remember motivation for yourself and your children is necessary if you are going to raise extraordinary kids.

 ## Idea File

🔊 BUY YOUR CHILDREN, *THE KID'S LITTLE INSTRUCTION BOOK* BY JIM AND STEVE DODSON

🔊 POST UP MOTIVATIONAL PICTURES AND BOOKS IN THEIR ROOM.

🔊 ASK YOUR CHILDREN QUESTIONS ABOUT SCHOOL, FRIENDS AND ACTIVITIES.

🔊 SPEAK TO YOUR KID'S POTENTIAL

🔊 PROVIDE A MOTIVATIONAL ATMOSPHERE WITH WORDS, MUSIC, BOOKS, TAPES AND THE BIBLE.

🔊 IF YOUR CHILDREN HAS FRIENDS THAT ZAP THEIR MOTIVATION, STIR THEM IN ANOTHER DIRECTION BY PERHAPS SUGGESTING TO THEM THEY SHOULD CHOOSE MORE UPBEAT FRIENDS.

Become a Better Mom

"It is pointless to appear to be a godly mother to the world if you are not loving and kind in your home."
- God's Tender Moments for Mothers

We need God's help to balance life's demands.

The Bible in Matthew 11:28, tells all who are weary and heavy laden to come to Him and he will give you rest. Whether you work inside or outside the home (or both), you are only human. God doesn't intend for us to do everything by ourselves, but rely on him for help. God can help you prioritize what's important in order for you to be a successful mother.

A women's role in the family is powerful.

Women carry a lot of influence in the shaping and developing of their children. As women we create the atmosphere and set the pace in our homes, so it's important that we keep our heart and mouth positive about our children. Proverbs 3:28 says, "Her children rise up and call her blessed; her husband also and he praiseth her." That's a good goal to strive for as a mother and wife.

The family is God's invention

He knows best how to make it work, and he cares about every

aspect of each family member's life. The best place to learn about how to raise your kids is from the Bible. A good church will teach on family matters and will value family relationships. Look for Christian tapes on the subject. Every year my husband and I will teach a series on marriage and family matters because parents need ongoing information and motivation to raise successful kids.

Every aspect of a woman's work is very significant. Whether we're changing a diaper or managing a staff, our work has dignity, honor and value before God. When you know your significance you'll have a positive attitude about being a mom.

Know What the Bible Says About Your Children

1. Proverbs 22:6- "Train up a child in the way he should go; and when he is old he will not depart from it."

2. Psalm 127:3-5 - "Lo children are an heritage of the Lord: and the fruit of the womb is his reward. As arrows are in the hand of a mighty man; so are children of the youth. Happy is the man that hath his quiver full of them: they shall not be ashamed, but they shall speak with the enemies in the gate."

3. Psalm 112:1-4 - "Praise ye Lord, Blessed is the man that feareth the Lord, that delighted greatly in his commandments. His seed shall be mighty upon earth. The generation of the upright shall be blessed. Wealth and riches shall be in his house: and his righteousness endureth forever. Unto the upright there ariseth light in the darkness: he is gracious, and full of compassion and righteous."

4. Proverbs 29:17 - "Correct thy son, and he shall give thee rest; yea, he shall give delight unto thy soul."

5. Proverbs 24:3 - "Through wisdom is an house built; and by understanding it is established:...."

6. Psalm 128:3 - "Thy wife shall be as a fruitful vine by the sides of thine house: thy children like olive plants round about thy table."

Did you know:
Our children are powerful instruments of His Spirit to be poured out for His purposes.

7. Proverbs 22:15 "Foolishness is bound in the heart of a child; but the rod of correction will drive it far from him." The rod is not identified as your hand or belt. The scriptural definition of the rod of correction is a flexible branch from a tree or stick.

8. Colossians 3:20-23 - "Children, obey your parents in all things: for this is well pleasing unto the Lord. Fathers provoke not your children to anger, lest they be discouraged. And whatsoever ye do, do it heartily, as to the Lord, and not unto men."

9. Proverbs 29:17 - "Correct thy son, and he shall give thee rest; yea, he shall give delight unto thy soul."

10. Proverbs 29:15 - "The rod and reproof give wisdom: but a child left to himself bringeth his mother to shame." Children need their mothers instructions and correction.

11. Proverbs 19:18 "Chasten thy son while there is hope, and let not thy soul spare for his crying."

12. I Samuel 3:13 (AMP) "And I now announce to him that I will his house forever for the iniquity of which he knew for his sons were bringing a curse upon themselves blaspheming God and he did not restrain them." God chose Abraham because he was faithful in his household. He rejected Eli because he didn't restrain his children.

Better Parenting Made Easy:
Tune In

Pay attention to your kids. Even if it means interrupting what you're doing from time to time. Be aware of your child's every day needs and listen to their dreams. Children go through different emotional growth spurts and they need your help through each one.

I listen to Ryan though he's very little. He still needs to know that he's saying something important. When you practice tuning in you also know what problems you're kids may be facing in life and you can guide them through them before you have a blow up. When my daughter Ariana was about five years old she was having a hard time sleeping in her room alone, and she would cry for hours if we left her with a baby-sitter to go out for an evening.

So I sat her down to talk to her about her behavior and I began by telling her that I knew how she felt. She blurted out, "No you don't because you never asked me, you never let me tell you what's wrong." Once I finally did listen, we resolved what was wrong with her and in no time she got over her crying spells when we were away. From that day forward I knew I had to tune in better and I began to really listen to my kids.

Get Enough Rest

Tuning in also means caring for yourself. If you're tired and stressed, you won't have the energy to tune in. Raising kids can be very tiring. If you're exhausted all the time, you will be resentful and insensitive. It's essential that you take out time for yourself. You can't wait for spare time; you have to plan it. You can get spurts of time alone if you have young kids and they take naps. You also need to get to bed on time yourself so you can wake up refreshed and energized.

Every week I take a day to go shopping because that's something I truly enjoy. I don't deprive myself of what makes me happy. You don't have to break the bank to go shopping for yourself every week. You can buy a book, makeup, body lotion, new underwear, or something else that makes you feel good about yourself. My husband encourages me to take a day to shop and have time to myself. Since I have been practicing my personal time ritual, I feel so refreshed. I'm always clearheaded and very content. Because I get enough rest it makes me a more productive wife, mother and leader.

Be Consistent

Children thrive on predictability. Schedules and rules give them a sense of order. It's so much easier for children to thrive if they have routines in their lives so they know when they get up, eat, take a nap, do home work, get dressed or go to bed, etc. Never be too lazy to enforce your routine and rules every time. Once your child knows you are serious about your methods they won't try to get you to bend them as often.

Stay Up-To-Date

In order to really understand your kids it's important that you stay up-to-date with their generation. Try to figure out what language they are talking, what clothes are in, what music they like, etc. Let them know it's important to you. Last summer a certain type of gym shoe was really hot and Ariana wanted a pair before school started. She had done so well  over the summer in her reading program that her Dad and I promised to get her a pair. What seemed like a simple promise turned into a three day journey looking for those shoes. My first thought was to tell her to settle for another type instead, but then I remembered that I had promised to get them, and it really meant a lot to her to be in style. We kept our word and it showed Ariana that we really are concerned about her interest.

Develop Yourself

Self-development is the best gift you can give to your family and kids. Luke 2:52 says that Jesus grew in four ways: in wisdom (intellectually), in stature (physically), in knowledge of God (spiritually), and in favor with man (socially and economically). God is interested in you living a well-rounded life. In order to be interesting to be around, you'll have to use your brain to stretch and grow. Take advantage of every learning opportunity. Attend your church women's conferences, and Bible studies, or enroll in a class. Always be reading something and listen to inspirational cassettes while cleaning, or cooking. E. Stanley Jones said, **"You don't grow old, you get old by not growing."** What can you do today to grow intellectually?

Pray for Your Children

Lamentations 2:19 tells you to, "Pour out your heart like water before the face of the Lord. Lift your hands toward him for the life of your young children." Your children's lives don't have to be left to chance. You can make a positive investment in their future by turning to God for help. Cover your kids in prayer and release them into God's hands. I have written confessions that I pray over my children concerning their problems and direction in life.

I think every mom should have a copy of Stormie Omartian's book *The Power of A Praying Parent*. It will give you step by step instructions on how to pray for any problem your kid may have no matter what their age.

 **Idea File**

✿ WHAT ARE THINGS YOU COULD YOU DO IMMEDIATELY TO BECOME A BETTER MOM.

✿ DO YOUR CHILDREN KNOW YOUR ROLES AND EXPECTATIONS? ARE YOU PREDICTABLE? CAN THEY COUNT ON YOU TO FOLLOW THE ROUTINE YOU HAVE SET FOR LIFE?

✿ SCHEDULE A DAY TO YOURSELF AT LEAST TWICE A MONTH AND DO EVERYTHING YOU CAN TO KEEP THE DATE. EVEN IF IT'S ONLY A FEW HOURS ALONE.

✿ UPDATE YOURSELF CONCERNING YOUR CHILDREN'S WORLD. FIND OUT WHAT FASHIONS, COLORS, ACCESSORIES, MUSIC, BOOKS AND LANGUAGES ARE IN.

Say "I Love You!"

SABRINA TODD

"Each loving act says loud and clear, I love you. God loves you. I care. God cares."
- Joyce Heinrich & Annette La Placa

"What the world needs now, is love sweet love..." That was a song that was made popular by Dionne Warwick several years ago. And what the world does need is love - God's love. But in order for God's love to be known in the world, it has to be known and shown in the home, especially with our children.

A parents' inability to show love results in the many dysfunctional and abrupt behaviors seen in the youth of today. With their suicides, school killings and gang violence young people are literally saying, " I want somebody to love me, to show me some significance.

Properly loving your child requires you to first love God. In Matthew 22:37-39 Jesus commanded, "Thou shalt love the Lord thy God will all thy heart, and with all thy soul and with all thy mind. This is the first and great commandment. And the second is like unto it, Thou shalt love thy neighbor as thyself." So can you see if we are to love God first and then our neighbor, then doesn't it behoove us to love our children?

You might even use the excuse that you weren't loved as a child yourself and think that excuses you from displaying love to your child. Not! God is love and He can show you how to love through his Word (I John 4:7-21). As the love of God abides and resides on the inside of you it will ultimately overflow into others, especially your children.

The most important thing to remember however is that your love must be sincere, genuine and consistent. Gary Chapman says in his book, *The Five Love Languages of Children*, **"Every child has an emotional tank, a place of emotional strength that can fuel him through the challenging days of childhood and adolescence... We need to fill our children's emotional tanks with unconditional love, because real love is always unconditional. Unconditional love is a full love that accepts and affirms a child for who he is, not for what he does."** There are countless other books available at your local library and bookstores that speak on loving your child, the following are just a few points to get you started.

Say "I love you" to your child with verbal words of affirmation.

Words spoken at the right time can mean so much, especially when spoken on a consistent basis. Affirmation spoken to your

100

child at different periods in their life will mean far greater to them later on in life than any other gift you can give them. Don't save the affirmation just for the private times, there are the appropriate times when you can verbally affirm them in public that won't cause them embarrassment.

Say I love you to your child with physical affection and contact.

I truly feel that "Love that isn't shown is love that will not be known." Give your child kisses and hugs. First of all understand that I'm speaking here of healthy, appropriate physical affection and contact, and not that of someone who is perverted in their ways. When our children were infants and toddlers, we kissed and hugged them frequently. We were always "in their face." Physical affection and contact on a regular basis gives your child a message of care and concern. However, you may notice that as your child gets older they may rebuff your acts of physical affection. Yet, if this frequency or constancy is not maintained (even in the face of their rebuffs) you may notice some distance in your relationship during their adolescent years.

It's also important to note that boys especially need the physical touch of their fathers or some significant male in their life as they grow up. The thinking that this shows weakness couldn't be further from the truth. On the contrary, this creates a strong and lasting bond between them that

101

aids in their proper growth. Our two sons (twenty one and eleven years old) have a very healthy and vital physical relationship with their father. They hug and kiss one another regularly and this does not bother them in any way. This has solidified their relationship into a very loving and trusting one.

"Physical touch is one of loves' strongest voices" Gary Chapman says again in his book *The Five Love Languages of Children*[1]. So, go ahead speak to your child in the strongest way possible. Kiss them, hug them. Love genuinely given is love genuinely received and reciprocated.

Say I love you to your child with appropriate discipline.

Proverbs tells us that, "He who spares the rod hates his son, but he who loves him is careful to discipline him" (Proverbs 13:24 NIV). Love is not never saying no to, or disciplining your child. Children need some loving boundaries. This establishes the necessary guidance and orderliness needed today. The plight of many youth is that of a lack of discipline. Therefore they are children (youth) left to their own devices with no direction or guidance.

In Hebrews 12:4-11 it speaks on how God disciplines us to show his love for us and how it makes us his true children. What more should we as Christian parents do for our children? Let me clarify, discipline is not abuse. Discipline is the correcting of a child's failure to obey your righteous command or instruction. We are commanded to train up our children in the way they should go, and when they are old they will not depart from it. (Proverbs 22:6) Correction and discipline given appropriately will direct the child

.

in the right way he/she goes especially as they grow older. It ensures their safety and their peace when the temptations of the world come against them. At that time they will have your teachings, training and discipline to refer to in order to make the right decision. Love your child enough to discipline them. Failure to discipline them is failure to love them.

Say I love you to your child with "Just Because" moments and quality time. Share special, private moments together with planned and spontaneous activity. Activities bring a closeness because of the interaction between those involved. With the many priorities placed upon us as parents our children need to know they can (and they should) have some time with us as well. They shouldn't be viewed as an interruption to our daily activities. Joining in with your child in an activity shows them that you care about their enjoyment and spending time with them.

Activities can range from visits to the library, bookstore, art gallery, museum, to a formal dinner, theater, plays, etc. When you are in card store buy them a card and send it to them (this is especially good when you are out of town on business trips). These are moments that your child will appreciate for years to come and keep them close in heart.

Do some "just because" celebrations for them. It doesn't have to necessarily be a special occasion to take your child out to dinner or the show or to buy them a gift. It oftentimes is the spontaneous that will really send a message of love to them. Most children come to expect the gifts and presents on their birthdays, Christmas, etc.. But watch the sparkle in their eye when you surprise them "Just Because". This will really register in their minds that, "my mom or my dad loves me."

Love is the greatest commandment given to man. "Love is patient, love is kind. It does not envy, it does not boast, it is not proud. It is not rude, it is not self-seeking, it is not easily angered, it keeps no record of wrongs. Love does not delight in evil, but rejoices with the truth. It always protects, always trusts, always hopes, always perseveres. Love never fails" (I Cor 13:4-8a NIV). Loving your child, tells your child that you celebrate them, and that they are significant to you. It speaks to every aspect of their being and who they are.

"In the end, nothing we do or say in this lifetime will matter as much as the way we have loved one another."
- Daphne Rose Kingma

 **Idea File**

♥ DO YOU SPEND ENOUGH TIME WITH YOUR KIDS? DOES YOUR SCHEDULE INCLUDE TIMES OF AFFECTIONATE INTERACTION WITH YOUR KIDS?

♥ SAY I LOVE YOU TO EACH OF YOUR KIDS TODAY.

♥ WRITE A LETTER TO YOUR CHILDREN WHO ARE OLD ENOUGH TO READ EXPRESSING YOUR GRATITUDE FOR THEIR LIVES AND TELLING THEM HOW MUCH YOU LOVE THEM.

♥ PLAN A JUST BECAUSE REWARD FOR EACH OF YOUR CHILDREN.

♥ GIVE YOUR CHILDREN THE SUPPORT OF YOUR LOVE, AND CONFIDENCE FOR THEIR INDIVIDUALITY.

14 Practice Listening

SABRINA TODD

" Children who are not listened to in the home live in a lonely silence. "

-Stan Wonderley

"Did you hear what I said?" How often have we responded to that question from our children with a causal "yes" or "huh, what did you say?" More often than we probably care to think.

Listening is quickly becoming a lost art. With everything else loudly clamoring for our attention, a real effort has to be made to listen, especially to our children. Our children need to know that what they say is being heard and being given attention. Because life has become too harried for most of us, many times our children give up trying to communicate with us and end up keeping issues to themselves. It is only when a major catastrophe occurs that many parents stop to listen. Then, it is often too late.

Listening to your child begins when they are babbling and rambling on as a small child and continues through their adolescent years until their teenage years when their conversation is filled with a lot of "ums", "uhs", and "you knows".

Why Listen?

We are assured through scripture that our heavenly Father listens to us. (Psalm 18:6, 116:1). The same thing applies to our children. They need to know that we as parents will hear them.

Listening shows care and concern for your child.

It shows them acceptance. It tells them that they and what they have to say is important. Watch how your child interacts with his/her friends, especially if they talk on the telephone. They are relating to someone who is listening to them. If your child favors spending an inordinate amount of their time with a particular friend or stays at that friend's house all the time, it could be because that friend and their family are listening to them. Children gravitate to where they feel accepted.

Listening reveals your child's interests.

Have you ever found out something about what your child was doing or something they liked, after the fact? And how did you respond? "I didn't know that?" That's because your child felt like someone else cared enough to listen to them and that's who they confided in. Being on the tail end of information regarding your child is like being in on the tail end of their life.

How Do You Listen?

Listen in an atmosphere of love with patience and an ear of wisdom. There will be times when it will be difficult for your child to tell you something or express how they are feeling. It is at these times that you may feel most vulnerable to respond with an impatient "hurry up I don't have all day." But it is important at these times to discern that your child is having difficulty in expressing himself. Do not treat what your child has to say as being silly or foolish. Make them feel comfortable. Fix them a cup of hot chocolate or tea. When your kids come to you with what may seem like a life or death issue to them, this is when they need an understanding ear, not an impatient one.

Listen for the "not so obvious" thoughts or expressions.

In other words listen "between the lines". There will be those times when your child seems to be talking nonsensically or in secret code. They are really trying to converse with you and they are using the conversation of the times or of their peers. Sometimes they really don't know how to express it, so listen for such phraseology as " I wonder what it's like..." or "it must be nice to.." They are hinting around at this point and you need to be aware in order to properly respond.

Listen by asking open ended questions.

Don't ask questions where they will reply with just a "yes" or "no". Ask them thought provoking questions using such phrases as, "What do you think about..", "How do you suppose..." These types of questions will elicit more than the one word responses.

Listen by looking at them.

Maintain eye contact with your child. Don't listen from behind a newspaper or while looking at television. Put the paper down, and turn the TV off. Stopping what you are doing shows your child that you are giving them your full attention.

Listen to your child while sharing some private activities together.

Private moments are the times when your child will feel secure and confident to open up to you. My youngest son and I have a night that we call Mother-Son night. He looks forward to this night and the minute I come in from work if something has not already been planned he usually asks what we will be doing.

We do things like going to dinner, the library, the movies, or just walking the mall. It is during these times that we talk and he shares with me about what is happening in his life.

Sharing private times together with your child also gives an opportunity for you to share with your child about your childhood and shows them that you may have experienced some of the same things they are going through (i.e. peer pressure, school, etc.).

Listen by respecting their privacy.

If your child tells you something that does not violate any spiritual or moral law be considerate enough not to betray their confidence or embarrass them. Many times your child will confide in you about personal issues dealing with their self esteem and they do not need the extra pressure, worrying about you relaying it onto someone else. Breaches of confidence such as this will close the lines of communication between you and your child.

Listen by letting them know that God will listen to them as well.

Psalm 50:15 says to "Call upon Him and he will hear." Your child needs the assurance of knowing that their Heavenly Father will listen to them, especially in those instances when no one else is available.

Benefits of Listening

Listening forms a special bond between you and your child(ren). They will know that you care, and that they can come to you about anything. Richard Carlson, in his book, *"Don't Sweat the Small Stuff...and It's All Small Stuff"*, says becoming a better listener enhances the quality of your relationships. A child who is heard

 saying, "I can talk to my parent(s) about anything", is a child whose parents listen to him.

Listening will give your child the needed confidence necessary for addressing life's issues as he/she grows up. They have an assurance of support for the important decisions they have to make while growing and maturing. It also teaches them to listen to you. This is very important. In Proverbs 4:20 God says for us to attend (listen) to Him. When you genuinely listen to your child you prepare the way for them to listen to you when you need to speak into their life.

Proverbs 22:6 admonishes parents to train up a child in the way that he should go...and part of that training will include listening.

111

Listening to your child isn't as difficult as it is made out to be. It takes time, yes, but it will be the most valuable time you've ever taken. Listen to your child today. Listening is vital to a child's growth and maturity. If you don't take the time now, someone else will and it could make all the difference in your relationship.

 **Idea File**

𝔇 THE GREATEST GIFT YOU CAN GIVE YOUR CHILD IS TO JUST LISTEN TO THEM. TODAY PRACTICE STOPPING WHAT YOU'RE DOING AND LISTENING TO YOUR CHILDREN.

𝔇 ASK YOUR CHILDREN QUESTIONS ABOUT WHAT THEIR DREAMS IN LIFE ARE AND LISTEN ATTENTIVELY.

𝔇 TUNE IN; LISTEN TO YOUR KID'S HINTS AND CONVERSATIONS WITH FRIENDS. YOU WILL PROBABLY DISCOVER SOME THINGS THEY HAVE BEEN TRYING TO TELL YOU.

Encourage Prayer & Bible Study

CATHY WRAY

"Prayer is an invisible tool which is wielded in a visible world."
- Leo Tolstoy

In a recent New York Times/CBS News poll of 1,048 teenagers, 94% said they believe in God, 7 in 10 believe in a God that participates actively in one's life. When asked what or who was the greatest influence in their life, religion was mentioned only second to parents. In a survey of 4,000 teens from across the country, the "successful" students said they gained strength and peace of mind from a higher source.[1]

Having a solid spiritual foundation can help young people avoid negative peer pressure. Because we are youth ministers, young people often share with my husband and I the temptations they face to have sex or use drugs. We have found that almost 100 percent of the time, a young person's ability to withstand temptation is directly related to the strength of their relationship with God. Successful teens have a strong relationship with God.

The spiritual well-being of our children should not be left to chance. It is up to us as parents to direct and shape our children's attitudes toward spiritual things.

Develop an Easy Method of Personal Bible Study

Of the many surveys we have conducted in our youth ministry over the years, the number one reason teenagers are not interested in reading the Bible is because they feel it does not relate to what they are facing in their life right now. Secondly, our young people never see that the Bible is affecting us in a positive way, so why should they bother?

As a parent of three teenagers, I realize that it is no small task getting teenagers to realize the importance of Bible study. In fact, most adults don't study the Bible on a regular basis for many of the same reasons that teens don't.

We decided to make Bible study exciting and relevant for our family. Last year for Christmas, we purchased new Bibles for everyone in the family and made it one of our family goals to read the Bible all the way through in one year. We purchased very readable versions of the Bible, so that we could all get understanding from our reading. The Bible is so remarkable. It doesn't matter if we're reading from the Old Testament or the New, we have always been able to relate something we have read in our Bible study to our everyday life.

For personal Bible study, each of our children read a chapter of Proverbs to correspond with the day of the month. From our family devotions, we give out personal Bible study assignments to each of our children. When we have family meetings they are able to expound on what they have read and how it has impacted their life. We also use everyday situations to create Bible study topics. One day our youngest daughter, Jasmine, was complaining about a sore throat. Even after we prayed for her, she kept proclaiming that she was still sick and in need of medication. You have to know Jasmine to know how dramatic a conflict she can create from the simplest situation. We finally gave Jasmine a personal bible study assignment to find out what the Bible says about healing and about her confession.

Establish Prayer Routines

Bible study and prayer go hand-in-hand. In order to pray effectively, we must know what the Bible says we can have or we end up wasting our time. It is up to us as parents to establish routines in the home. Remember, our young people will usually pattern their lifestyle after us.

Every morning my husband and I and our three teenagers join hands and pray before we leave for work or school. We follow a prayer list we developed that includes specific things that we felt should be covered in prayer each day. At first, my husband would lead the prayer each day, but eventually he assigned one day for each child to lead the prayer. They resisted having to lead initially, but as we continued to stress the importance of acknowledging God and not being ashamed of relating to Him in prayer, each of them have grown accustomed to praying in a public setting.

One of our greatest desires has always been for our children to work alongside us in ministry. We try to encourage their participation by making sure that they receive the benefits promised in the Word of God. Each time their prayers work, they gain a new confidence in God and acquire boldness to witness to their friends for Christ.

Last year our oldest daughter, Nikki, wanted to go out for cheerleading. Having been a cheerleader for several years while in high-school I felt I could spot cheerleading talent when I saw it, and Nikki simply didn't have it. In an effort not to discourage her, I simply told her to pray about try outs. Maybe God could help her make the squad - so we did.

Nikki and her tryout partner practiced diligently every evening. When the day of tryouts came Nikki decided to fast. Her tryout partner did not profess Christianity at the time, but Nikki suggested that she fast also - and she did. When the list was posted with the names of the new cheerleaders, sure enough, Nikki and her partner's names were on the list. She actually made the squad!

Because Nikki challenged God by using His Word, she got exactly the results she was expecting. Her tryout partner ended up becoming a regular at our youth services along with more than half of her entire squad.

Prayer, Bible Study & Family Traditions

Studies show that families who attend church often have children with a higher level of emotional wellness than children from families that did not attend church together.

Not only should going to a good Bible-believing church together, be a family tradition in your home, but you should also establish certain monumental events that fit the lifestyle of your family and incorporate prayer, bible study and recognition of God. Yearly goal setting is one of our family traditions, that we learned from our pastors. Each year around Christmas time, our family comes together to determine what our next year will be like. We review our former year's goals and talk about which goals we accomplished and which ones we didn't. We set goals in five areas: personal, career, spiritual, educational, and financial; we use the Bible to gauge what our end results should be. Each of us develop personal goals and together we develop a family mission.

Because we've established this practice in our household we can look forward to the tradition of honoring and acknowledging God for each new year, being passed onto our grandchildren and the generations after them.

 **Idea File:**

KEEP THE FAITH: THE MOST SUCCESSFUL TEENS HAVE A STRONG RELATIONSHIP WITH GOD.

📖 PURCHASE AN EASY TO READ BIBLE MOST TEENS DON'T READ IT BECAUSE THEY DON'T UNDERSTAND IT.

📖 ESTABLISH PRAYER AND BIBLE STUDY TIMES

📖 SET PRAYER GOALS

📖 MAKE THE BIBLE RELEVANT TO YOUR KIDS TODAY

Promote A Good
16 Body Image

"When you feel good about yourself on the inside you will sparkle on the outside!"

- The Care And Keeping Of You

Parents should take a look at their own behavior before they can offer genuine advice to their kids.

What messages are you sending about your image? Are you always on a self-esteem, emotional roller coaster, complaining about your weight, eating lots of junk food, and going through bouts of depression? If that's the case you must first deal with your own self-image in order to help your son or daughter. Be a good role model for your kids and take care of you. Then show them how to take care of themselves.

Strengthen your relationship with each one of your children. Strong parental support always gives a child more confidence in themselves. During a child's adolescent years puberty embarks upon them and it's very crucial time in their life. They are coming to all sorts of conclusions about their bodies and their worth. You should guide them through these years with lots of support and encouragement. Instead, most mothers back away and let their kids grow up on their own.

Stay In Touch

Parents should know what's going on in their kids' lives to the point where they can recognize changes - positive or negative, when they see them.

Know What Goes On In School

Check for signs of harmful name calling or problems with friends. Also visit your child's school from time to time throughout the year. You'll see first hand how the kids act. Ask your kids daily "What happened at school today? Is there anything you'd like to share with me?"

Be the First To Talk about Sex With Your Kids

Kids emerging sexually can be both confusing and exciting to them. Don't leave it up to the school sex education classes to teach your kids. Some of the films they show and talks they give are very inappropriate. In most schools they are telling the kids how to have safe sex instead of how to abstain from sex.

Resources for Parents about Discussing Sex

What's the Big Secret. Talking about sex with girls and boys by Lanie Kransny Brown and Mark Brown. (Little Brown, 1997. $15.95) Ages 4-10

Where Did I Come From? The facts of life without any nonsense with illustrations by Peter Mayle. (Carol Publishing Group) 1997. $9.95 Ages 6-10

The What's Happening To My Body Book for Girls and the *What's Happening to My Body Book for Boys.* Both by Lynda Madaras (New Market Press 1993) $11.95 Ages 10 and up. I recommend you don't just give these books to your kids, but rather go through them with your kids, explaining and inputting your own views and values.

Set Clothing Guidelines

Kids should be kept up-to -date in their clothing styles, but there should be limits to what they wear. I want my children to exemplify a Christian character, and some clothing styles are too revealing, so there not allowed to wear those styles. Kids also have to be taught to dress appropriate for certain occasions. If you are dining at a very nice restaurant and you are dressing up a bit, then the kids should do likewise. Don't allow them the option of wearing jeans, because then we teach them to rebel against social rules. If you have a child who expresses they like to pick out their own clothes then solve the dilemma by giving them a choice between two outfits.

Have your older school age kids pick out their clothes the night before and get them ready so they don't have clothing disasters right before school in the morning. What your child looks like will determine how people will judge them. So buy them clothes that aren't too tight, form-fitting, revealing, droopy looking, or ill fitting, meaning the wrong look for their body type.

Teach them Clothes Care

Children gain esteem when they learn to care for their clothing by hanging up their clothes instead of throwing them on the floor. Keeping clothes clean is important; dirty smelly clothes are a sign of carelessness.

Promote Good Hygiene

First provide all the information your kids need about proper hygiene and then provide all the tools- deodorant, soap, toothpaste, mouthwash, tooth brushes, floss, feminine pads if necessary, facial cleansers, body lotions, powders, perfumes and colognes. Often when you give each child their own personal hygiene tools they take ownership of their image. Boys may need extra encouragement in this area, but they need to be taught to care for their bodies just like girls. Often boys don't like bathing or flossing their teeth because they think hygiene tasks are really for girls. Teach your kids that when they take care of their bodies they are showing respect for their bodies.

When I wanted to introduce my daughter to good hygiene, I bought her a Caboodles makeup holder and filled it with personal hygiene products. Then I purchased a few books on personal hygiene and included it in the kit. One of the most recent books I bought for Ariana was, *The Care And Keeping Of You*, by the American Girls Library[1] This is a great book for girls ages 8-15. I was so impressed with the contents that I bought several copies and gave them away for Christmas presents. Next I went through all the products with Ariana, explaining their use and importance to her looking and feeling good.

Encourage Rest

To be healthy and fit a child's body needs plenty of rest. Sleeping is the body's way of recharging itself. Set a regular bedtime schedule for your kids. I heard one CEO of a very prosperous company said, everyone in his family including, himself, goes to bed by 9:00p.m. unless he's away traveling, they all arise at 5:00 a.m. All of his kids have grown up to be super productive. Routines always give stability to a child. Try to get your older kids to develop their own bedtime ritual like taking a bath, writing a journal entry, then going to sleep. For younger kids you can develop their ritual for them.

Practice Good Eating Habits

Provide healthy snacks in the house, like apples, pears, all sorts of fruits and fresh vegetables. If you buy the groceries you can control what your family eats. Poor nutrition will not only result in overweight kids but can also hinder their brain power, zap kids of all their energy and in some cases cause depression or hypertension. Many kids on Ritalin, when tested by nutritionists, were found to be normal kids, just with too much sugar intake or an overdose of "non nutritional" foods like hot dogs or lunch meats. A good breakfast is key to a child's attentiveness throughout the day. Many times kids lack energy and their immune systems are low just because they never drink water. A common thread found in kids who developed chronic diseases like cancer is that they never drink pure water and they consume a lot of junk foods and soda pop.

Harvard Medical School researchers evaluated 86 children before and after they were enrolled in a national school breakfast program. After four months in the program, students were much more attentive, received higher math grades, and had fewer behavioral and emotional problems. Although these children were from low income families, the results make sense for all kids, says Ronald Kleinman M.D., a study author.

For quick, nutritious breakfasts try yogurt and granola cereal, bananas and a bran muffin, whole wheat toast with fresh fruit, quick oatmeal with real butter and honey or a smoothie made with a frozen banana and strawberries, a little ice and orange juice, blended in your blender. Good nutrition will result in smarter, happier and healthier children. For more information get my book, *A Christian Woman's Guide to Health and Nutrition* and *Food Smart* by Cheryl Townsley (Pinon Press).[2] What your kids eat will have a direct effect on their ability to learn and achieve.

Offer Inspiration

Watch your words. Never tell your child they look funny or they're fat. Not only do these kind of words pierce their hearts, it also fosters a negative self image from the people they care about the most. Laughing at your kids is another image killer that causes them to draw back from anything that challenges them for fear of failure. You can give critical feedback along with praise. Try a comment like, "By keeping your clothes clean all week you really showed maturity."

 Idea File

- Have your children exercise with you. Take them bike riding, to the gym, do aerobics, run together.

- Don't allow you kids to eat whatever they want. My kids are no different from yours. They would eat junk food all the time if I let them.

- Do a refrigerator and pantry check. What type of foods are you stocking your shelves with?

- Use this week to offer inspiration to each of your kids every chance you get!

17 Turn off the TV

"The television is robbing our kids of their creativity."
-Stacia Pierce

Turn off the TV and instead turn on the talk. It's so hard to have real interactive conversation while the TV is on. When you stop talking to catch a scene or to laugh at a commercial. Your conversation becomes shallow chitchat.

When the TV is turned off, the house suddenly becomes serene. Then your family fills the house with noise. You'll be amazed at what your kids will find to do when watching TV is not an option. They will be more inclined to grab a book, play a game, write or draw, or talk. Just the other day I was home with my two children and I said OK, turn off the TV, our television time is over. A few moments later while I was sitting at the kitchen table thumbing through a new book, my one year old made up some game with his shoes that were sitting by the door. He began to pretend like they were cars and push them all across the floor. My daughter went and grabbed her book, pulled up a chair next to mine and finished her book. Then she got out her markers and began to draw. I thought to myself, "if they were watching TV, until it was time for bed, they would of been deprived of being so creative today."

It is possible that by the time the average high school student graduates from high school they will have spent 15,000 to 18,000 hours in front of the television compared to 12,000 hours in the classroom. Television watching is second only to sleeping when it comes to occupying childhood leisure time. It's been said that 33% of all US children watch four or more hours of television each day. On any given night it is estimated that more that 20 million children age two to seventeen are watching television between the hours of 7:00 pm and 11:00 pm.

Those are alarming numbers, but very real in our teen culture. If parents don't step in and take an active role in monitoring their children's TV viewing then we are bound to end up with youth who are lazy, nonsocial, lack creativity and even possibly violent.

Television viewing can have a profound impact on a child's development. Studies have shown that too much television viewing can actually be addictive for children and promote other various negative behaviors such as: childhood obesity, substance abuse, racial stereotypes and decreased interest in reading. Experts believe that too much TV has affected creativity, basic language skills, and school achievement in our children.

Even television shows we've believed to be educational like Barney and Sesame Street have their limitations. Teachers believe that real learning for children is not passive, but involves hands on interaction and discussion. Children learn what they live. So you have to be a living example in the home. Don't tell them

to limit TV but you watch several hours of it yourself. Usually kids claim for watching TV is that they are bored. So give them ideas for alternative ways to use their time; then allow for creative play.

Suggest they read a book, complete some chores, play a game or work on one of their goals. Set some TV guidelines. Limit the amount of TV they can watch in a week. We set our guideline for eight hours in a week with the exception of going to a show on a weekend. Know what your kids are watching. Don't leave them in a room by themselves for hours to watch whatever they wish. Get your kids involved in after school activities, specialty courses or sports, which are excellent alternatives.

If your family isn't already on some sort of TV plan then sit down with your kids and explain why you're making these positive changes in their TV viewing. Once they hear about how concerned you are about their future they will be more adaptable to the changes.

 **Idea File**

☐ TAKE A TV FAST FOR A WEEK AND CHALLENGE YOUR KIDS TO FILL THE TIME BEING CREATIVE AND COMMUNICATING.

☐ MAKE A TV CHART OF WHAT PROGRAMS YOUR KIDS CAN AND CANNOT WATCH. ALSO ALLOT AN AMOUNT OF TV THAT CAN BE VIEWED IN A WEEK.

☐ DON'T GET CAUGHT UP IN THE HOME VIDEO TRAP. FIND ANOTHER ACTIVITY FOR WEEKENDS, BESIDES RENTING A HOME MOVIE.

☐ IF YOU HAVE TEENS WHO ARE HOME ALONE EACH DAY FOR LONG PERIODS OF TIME, ASK THEM WHAT THEY ARE WATCHING ON TV AND SET GUIDELINES.

18 Let Them Entertain Themselves

"Tis better to be alone than in bad company."
-Oliver Wendell Holmes

When a child says I'm bored that can be a good thing. You needn't wear yourself out trying to find something to keep them busy. Your children can benefit from a little solo time. Children who grow up that can create their own fun will wind up being more independent and well balanced. Often children who grow into adults who do extraordinary things, were allowed to have solo time and to be creative. Keep a stash of supplies around the house so they can have creative play. I always make sure there are new books, stamps, colored markers, stickers, construction paper, paint and children's computer games in our home.

Give them creative challenges.

Some kids need to have a specific goal to work toward. While the kids were off from school I set up a schedule of little projects for my daughter and her friends to do. One day I had her make greeting cards from her computer program which sparked the idea for a card business. You can also suggest your kids make a collage or use a camera to take photographs of things that interest them.

Encourage outdoor play.

Young children as well as teenagers can find creative play out

133

doors. There is so much to do, from riding bikes, to playing basketball, playing with dolls, climbing in a treehouse, swinging, tennis, soccer, laser tag, golfing, sledding or roller-blading. There is no excuse to just allow kids to plop down in front of the TV and declare that there's nothing to do. Turn off the TV and watch how quickly they find some sort of creative play. Television can be mesmerizing. It puts an end to all activities, so you wind up with a kid who doesn't know how to initiate playing on his own.

Post a list of things to do.

You can post chores that need to be done during the week. As well as activities that should be done like thank you cards, letters to pen pals, homework assignments, book reports, science projects, practicing instruments, writing in a journal, washing clothes, etc.

Let them make a mess.

Often the most interesting and educational activities are the ones that make the biggest messes. Things like cooking, painting, building, or making science projects are very messy, but these could be practice for the world's next builder, artist, inventor or explorer. So allow a little mess in order to stir up your child's creativity.

 **Idea File**

A List of Boredom Buster for Kids by Kids

SOME IDEAS ARE MY OWN, OTHERS ARE FROM KIDS I INTERVIEWED TO SEE WHAT THEY THOUGHT WAS FUN TO ENTERTAIN THEMSELVES.

PREPARE A SNACK. USE A CREATIVE KID'S COOK BOOK TO MAKE A FUN SNACK.

PLAY DRESS UP. YOUNGER OR OLDER KIDS ENJOY CHANGING CLOTHES AND SEEING WHAT OUTFITS WORK.

LISTEN TO MUSIC. DURING THEIR PRIVATE TIME OR DURING TIME WITH FRIENDS ALLOW THEM TO PLAY THEIR MUSIC KIND OF LOUD.

CUT PICTURES FROM MAGAZINES. CUT OUT PICTURES OF THINGS THEY LIKE FROM MAGAZINES AND MAKE POSTER BOARD COLLAGES.

WRITE A SHORT STORY OF POEM. NOT FOR SCHOOL, JUST FOR FUN.

PLAY BASKETBALL OR FOOTBALL. GET A TEAM OF GUYS TOGETHER AND GO TO A LOCAL PARK AND PLAY SPORTS ALL DAY.

TALK ON THE PHONE. CALL A FRIEND AND TALK ABOUT FUN STUFF.

READ A BOOK. READ AN EXCITING AND ADVENTUROUS BOOK THAT YOU HAVE BEEN TRYING TO CATCH UP ON.

PLAY THE SONY PLAYSTATION.

JOURNALIZE. WRITE ABOUT YOUR DAY'S ADVENTURES, COLOR IN YOUR JOURNAL OR CREATE NEAT FASHION DESIGNS.

MEDITATE ON GOD. USE THE BIBLE OR DEVOTIONAL BOOKS TO READ AND WRITE NOTES IN YOUR JOURNAL.

WORK ON THE COMPUTER OR LINK ONTO THE INTERNET. PLAY ON THE COMPUTER WITH COMPUTER GAMES DESIGNED FOR KIDS.

CONDUCT A PLAY WITH FRIENDS.

PLAY LASER TAG

WRITE LETTERS TO PEN PALS AND FRIENDS, THEN DECORATE THE ENVELOPES WITH STICKERS AND DRAWINGS.

Take Exciting Vacations and Spend Quality Time Together

" Take vacations that will upgrade your lifestyle while giving you the pleaure of relaxing. "

-Stacia Pierce

When I was a child my family took three exciting vacations that were impactful to me. The memory of the summer we went to Disneyland in California is still fresh in my mind. I was awe struck by all the life size characters that I saw in person. Then touring the live sets of Hollywood movie studios enlarged my vision for life. Walking down Rodeo Drive and actually being able to buy a thing or two set me on a new course in life. My ten year old mind came to the conclusion that I would grow up and do something extraordinary to impact my world.

When my husband and I created our family mission we decided that our vacations must be a part of our family tradition. One of the greatest things about vacationing is that they bond families. I believe it's the combination of quality time and quantity time from the normal routines that allow for serious and funny conversations. Plus you may notice things about one another that you have overlooked in your day to day settings.

Because my daughter is old enough to make mature decision of what's fun we include her in our vacation planning. I began buying books about different states and unique places around the world for Ariana when she was about six years old. I have a collection of free brochures from many Chamber of Commerce around the country. I would have Ariana read these books and look at the brochures so she could make an educated decision about some of the places she wanted to visit. I'll never forget bringing her the book, *My New York* by Kathy Jakobsen,[1] from one of the week long New York shopping excursions with my husband. Ariana was delighted with the book , because it brought New York to life for her. Actually I was very inspired by the book myself. The book stirred my daughter so much that she couldn't get the idea of vacationing in New York out of her mind.

Well, the next year we teamed up with another family and took our kids on a East Coast vacation tour. It was one of the best family vacations we have ever had. When kids experience new places, cultures and different people it gives them a broader view of their world. I think it stifles a child's imagination and ability to develop when you limit their family vacation to visiting their same relatives every year.

Family vacations can get expensive so they have to be well planned; plus you want the experience to be a pleasurable one. Maybe some of the following tips can aid you in planning a wonderful vacation your family won't forget.

Pick A Destination

Include the kids in the planning. Ask whether they would like to go to the beach, camping, Disneyland, on a cruise or skiing. Then work within your means to design a trip everyone will enjoy.

Decide How You Will Travel

Driving, renting a camper, bus, train, or plane? We decided last year to rent a van for our East Coast vacation because we could do and see more, even along the way to our destination. Book your reservations and seat assignments well in advance if you're traveling by plane, otherwise you may have difficulty getting seated together.

Start a Vacation Fund

Write out a vacation budget. Count up all the costs you can possibly think of. Open a savings account designated for vacation money only. Weekly make a deposit into the account.

Pray Over Your Trip

Long before it's time to leave, paste up your brochures and pictures and began as a family to pray for a safe trip. Pray for favor and bargains. Also pray for peace and bonding among everyone.

Reserve Your Hotel Rooms or Lodging Place

Get confirmation numbers and names of the people you talk to. Find a family-friendly hotel to stay in. Most hotels have indoor swimming, workout rooms and nice gift shops for your convenience.

Take a Photo Journal and Camera

Family memories are captured when you take lots of pictures. I brought Ariana her own camera so she can capture what is important to her. As soon as we arrived home last summer from

139

our vacation, we developed the pictures and spent two days putting together our photo journal while the memories were still fresh.

Bring Your Books

Retrieve to an isolated spot, and have an adventure all your own. Early in the morning I usually escape to a patio or pool-side lounger to bask in the sun and catch up on some reading.

Pack Right

Don't pack clothes for yourself or your family that you never wear at home, chances are you won't feel comfortable in them on vacation either. Allow your young children to help with packing and tell your older children to make a list before they pack. You should narrow down your chances of forgetting something. Your family vacation can be an exciting experience when planned well. So make your very next vacation a great adventure.

Make Dinner Time Family Time

If your family runs anything like ours this suggestion could seem like a fairy-tale. It is possible that up to 62% of Americans call their supper hour "hectic". In most homes today both parents and kids are involved in many activities. But a little bit of  togetherness can greatly enhance your relationship with your children.

Sunday is our big family / eating together day. We usually come home from church and have dinner together, sharing and laughing without any other distractions like the TV. Sometimes we don't even answer the phone during dinner time; not only does your food get cold, but the interruption can take your mind completely off of enjoying your family. Eating together demonstrates to everyone the importance of family time, despite how busy everyone can get. Sitting down to share a meal, a laugh, or a story sends a message to kids that the family is a top priority even if you can only do it once a week.

During our family mealtime I like to create a festive atmosphere. I use candles, fresh flowers, and other center pieces to decorate the table. I use my best dishes; sometimes it's bright colorful plates or china and crystal. We engage in meaningful conversation. This is not a time where we tell the kids to be quiet, instead we tug on them to talk. I have collected a few family mealtime ideas that will make any dinner exciting. If coordinating dinner is an unobtainable goal, perhaps try breakfast, this could be a real good time of positive impartation before your kids go off to school.

Overall family dinners tend to be more nutritious when kids are not left on their own to fix dinner . They tend to grab high fat snacks, instead of a well balanced nutritious meal. Even if you can't physically be home to cook dinner every night, provide a healthy menu for your kids. Personally I don't cook everyday; but I try to keep the refrigerator stocked with healthy snacks.
If you have smaller children use dinner as a time to teach and reinforce good eating habits and table etiquette.

The best way to get started in having a family meal time is to pick one day for a sit down meal together and stick to it. Next inform the entire family of your day and time. Rather than taking a vacation or having a meal with your family, it's being together that counts. Your kids will truly appreciate you taking out time to make memorable occasions.

Have a "Describe Your Day" Time

Go around the table having everyone describe the best thing and the most challenging thing that happened that day.

Kid's Pick

Once a week allow one of your children to choose what you will have for dinner and the topic of discussion. After the family eats dinner together share a Bible story with the whole family and discuss it over dessert.

Special Plate Day

Have a special plate in silver or gold, and once a week one of the members of your family gets to eat off that plate and all other family members have to tell them something special about them-selves.

 **Idea File**

PICK A DESTINATION YOU WOULD LIKE TO GO WITH YOUR CHILDREN. CALL THE CHAMBER OF COMMERCE IN THAT STATE AND GET A VISITOR'S PACKET.

BUY YOURSELF A TRAVEL JOURNAL TO DOCUMENT ALL OF YOUR EXCITING ADVENTURES. YOU WILL HAVE VALUABLE INFORMATION FOR YOUR CHILDREN WHEN THEY'RE GROWN.

CREATE A FESTIVE ATMOSPHERE FOR THE NEXT DINNER WITH YOU FAMILY. ADD A SPECIAL TOUCH AND USE CANDLES, FRESH FLOWERS, AND YOUR BEST PLATES.

Teach Music Matters

SABRINA TODD

"Music is a sound investment for life"

-Sabrina Todd

Music is the universal language of the heart and soul.

It is that which speaks straight to the very depths of ones being. "Music has the ability to express what is often hard to say. It opens up the spirit to receive whatever is intended by the human soul", says Lorin Hollander in *Music and Miracle*.

Music finds its' very existence with God where it was used in worship unto God.

The harmony, lyrics and rhythms of music that we now know and hear today have evolved over time from its beginnings. It has evolved for the most part into types and styles that have their own particular audience and it is these audiences that man has used music to convince, manipulate and energize through the years.

Music has long been touted for its therapeutic benefits.

When King Saul was being tormented by evil spirits David would play on his harp and the relief would come. Music is now a recognized therapy used in hospitals and nursing homes and has become a part of school curriculum on college campuses. As parents we need to allow music (and the appreciation of it) to be a part of our home environment. Music broadens a child's horizon of the fine arts and opens up their creativity.

Music matters in your child's life when they play an instrument

Many child's involvement in music begins with their taking up some type of instrument at a young age. Enroll them in private lessons, or allow them to become a part of the school band or orchestra. (Note: A school band or orchestra also allows them to be able to understand what it is like to be a team member.) Involving your child in music  by taking him to the theater, musicals, plays etc. gives them an appreciation for music in its finer style. With many of the heavy metal, rock and ghetto rap that is widely luring our youth, they need to see music at its pure and simple form, and most often this happens by taking them to the play or to the symphony.

Your child may balk at first if you take them to a symphony but if you explain it to them and allow them to continue to experience it, as with anything, they will eventually begin to appreciate it. Check out your local paper for upcoming musicals, plays, etc. You will usually find a lot of them being conducted around the holidays, and this is a good time to take them.

Exposing your child to music doesn't have to be something on a grand scale nor do they have to be a musical prodigy. The simple pleasures in life are sometimes as simple as a song. Music can be that avenue that can enable the heart and soul to breathe a song all its own.

Music will matter in your child's life when you sing and let them listen to music. Singing to and around your child has benefits of its own. It has long been used in the teaching arena in allowing the memory to retain what was vital for knowledge. How many children today would not know their alphabet, their numbers or how to tie their shoes or button their jacket if it weren't for the little ditties they learned in school and even on shows like Sesame Street, or The Electric Company? Even some of you now still remember those tunes.

I have been singing ever since I was a small child. My whole family would gather and sing around the house especially during the holidays. We would sing on long car trips. Oftentimes songs would be made up on the spur of the moment. I was also involved in school choirs during my junior high and high school years. My appreciation for music increased as a result of this. Sing around your child. Let him hear you sing especially songs of worship to God, this will enable him to be able to worship God. Allowing your child to hear you sing also allows them to see that side of you that is special and at times private.

147

I composed a lullaby song for my youngest son when he was an infant that I sang to him during those nights when he was fussy. I sing that song to him now at night on an occasion. It brings back those quiet tender moments when he was a small baby.

Let your child listen to music as well. Buy them their own stereo system and their own CD's or tapes so they are not always intruding upon yours. There are many styles of good music out there (jazz, rap, classical, hip-hop, praise & worship, gospel, etc.). If you begin buying music for them as a small child and if you train them on the right music and lyrics to listen to, the  probability of them being hooked on the wrong kind will be very minimal if not zero.

My dad had a collection of recordings of symphonic movements by the great composers (Beethoven, Mozart, Schubert, Tchaikovsky, etc.) He would sometimes play them hours on end and the intensity of the songs and the various instruments would literally be refreshing and exhilarating. This exposure has carried over into my adulthood. I have classical music playing in the background of my office. I'm also the worship leader for my church.

I can remember attending musicals as a young child and being involved at times, with their production. Involving your child by taking them to the theater, musicals, plays etc. gives them an appreciation for music in it's finer style. Your child may balk at first if you take them to the symphony, but if you explain it to them and allow them to continue to experience it, as with anything else, they will learn to appreciate it.

Exposing your child to music doesn't have to be something on a grand scale, and they don't have to be a musical prodigy. The simple pleasures in life are sometimes as simple as a song. Music can be that avenue that can enable the heart and soul to breathe a song all it's own. Remember, music won't matter to your child, until *you* make it matter.

 ## Idea File:

♪ TAKE YOUR CHILDREN TO A LIVE MUSICAL PERFORMANCE.

♪ INVEST IN QUALITY MUSIC FOR YOUR CHILDREN. TAKE A TRIP TO YOUR LOCAL CHRISTIAN BOOKSTORE WITH YOUR KIDS AND LET THEM CHOOSE SOME TUNES.

♪ HAVE YOUR CHILDREN TAKE MUSIC LESSONS AT LEAST ONCE IN THEIR LIFE.

Make Them Mind Their Manners

"Manners are a sensitive awareness of the feelings of others. If you have that awareness, you have good manners, no matter what fork you use."

- Emily Post

Having manners is simply displaying friendliness, kindness, sensitivity and empathy. Ultimately good manners reflect good values. Children are not born with good manners, they must be taught. It takes repetition, discipline, and modeling to raise kids with good manners.

American kids today seem to have a lack of manners. The primary source of a child's learning of manners has to come from teaching it at home. Manners is too big of a task to leave to school teachers. In a recent survey only 12% of 2,000 adults polled felt that kids commonly treat others with respect; most described them as rude, irresponsible and lacking in discipline. Just 19% believed that parents provided good role models or helped their kids know right from wrong. Most parents want to raise compassionate and civil children, but just have not taken the time to do so. In order to raise emotionally intelligent kids they must obtain skills in understanding and getting along with others.

13 Ways to Prepare Your Kids for Social Occasions

"Politeness goes far, yet costs nothing." -
Descartes

1. Say Thank You

Thank you is one of the most appreciated manner words. It makes others feel good about what they have done for you. Kids should be reminded to say thank you when they get a compliment or someone does them a favor. Anytime a child visits another friend's home and they eat dinner there or spend the night they should thank the host for having them over. Of course saying thank you is also appropriate when a gift is received.

When to have your kids write a thank you card:
* When someone gives them a present
* When they have been a house guest
* When someone has done them a favor
* After a dinner party or luncheon
* At the end of the school year (thanking their teachers)

2. Respond to an R.S.V.P.

When invited to an event RSVP is an abbreviation for the french words that mean "respond if you please". This enables the host to have specific numbers to prepare for her guests. Therefore, it is essential to respond by the deadline date.

3. When Invited to a Birthday Party Bring a Gift

It's common courtesy to bring a present to the honored guest, even if you have to make a gift by baking cookies or making a special card. Always bring something.

4. Teach Your Kids to Celebrate Others

It's good manners to be happy for the honored guest at a party if they receive gifts. One year at my daughter's party one of her guests began pouting when she began unwrapping her presents. Then the little girl went in another room, folded her arms and wouldn't participate with the other kids. I told her she was demonstrating bad manners and should learn to be happy for others when it's their time to receive.

5. Mealtime Manners

At the table the kids should behave in a way that everyone can enjoy their food and company. Kids should be taught to always wash their hands before eating. Home training on how to set a table and what silverware to use first is good. A good book on manners is called *Elbows Off the Table, Napkins in the Lap; No Video Games during Dinner* by Carol Wallace

6. Bathroom Manners

Flushing the toilet and washing your hands after using the restroom should be common among kids, but its not and even some adults miss a beat when it comes to bathroom etiquette. If your children ever leave from the bathroom without flushing the toilet and washing send them back in there to take care of their private business.

7. Telephone Manners

Have your children practice the art of smiling when they pick up the phone to say hello. Remind them that "who is it, yeah," or "whaddaya want?" are not appropriate ways to answer the phone. Limit phone conversations. Being considerate about using the phone means not talking too long, taking up other people's time and hindering others from incoming or outgoing calls.

8. Play Manners

I make sure that when my children and their friends play games they do so fairly. When your kids know that you're both concerned about their actions and that you're watching them, they'll watch their behavior carefully.

9. Say Hello and Good Bye

Sometimes kids don't say hello because they don't know how to introduce themselves. If they meet someone for the first time their response should be, "Hello, my name is _____". When it's time to go simply saying good-bye is good manners.

10. Teach Your Kids to Listen in Class

Many times kids get into trouble at school for talking in class. It's usually because they haven't been taught that it's bad manners to talk when someone else is supposed to be talking. When parents convey the consequences for talking in school as serious, kids will be more be reluctant to talk. My father used to quote a saying to me, "As long as you're talking, you're not learning." Talking too much is a big hindrance in some kids' learning abilities. The punishment for talking too much shouldn't be taken lightly. Every year before school starts, go over behavioral standards you expect from your kids and lay out some punishments if they don't comply. For example, punishments could include: no sports involvement, no after school activities, no phone calls, etc.

11. Waiting Politely

Oftentimes kids forget who's in charge and they begin to direct their parents as to when it's time to leave. It's OK for a child to say politely, "Can we go now?" or "I'm ready to go", but when a child is old enough to know better - tugging, whining, tantrums or yelling out, "I want to go home!" is inappropriate. Most of the time the kids need to be disciplined on the spot so they know that sort of behavior is unacceptable.

12. Say "Excuse Me"

When your kids bump into someone they should say, "Excuse me" or "I'm sorry".

13. Teach your Children to Apologize When They've Done Something Wrong.

 **Idea File**

☐ GIVE YOUR KIDS EMILIE BARNES BOOK, LITTLE MISS MANNERS

☐ AMERICAN GIRL-PLEASANT COMPANY HAS A BOOK CALLED: OOPS! THE MANNERS GUIDE FOR GIRLS (1997)

☐ PURCHASE THE MAN IN DEMAND CHARM COURSE BY HUNTER FOR YOUR SON(S). AVAILABLE THROUGH BAKER BOOKHOUSE IN GRAND RAPIDS, MI 1-616-957-3110

☐ REVIEW THE PREVIOUS LIST OF MANNERS WITH EACH AGE APPROPRIATE CHILD.

Enjoy Activities With Your Kids

CATHY WRAY

"Children have never been very good at listening to their elders, but they have never failed to imitate them."

- James Baldwin

As parents, it is important that we never stop growing and learning new things. The best way for parents to become motivated to learn is simply to spend time with their children. Studies show that the most important indicator of a child's success in school and in life is parental involvement. Parental participation in a child's life has the ability to influence more than teacher-to-student or student-to -student relationships. A study conducted by Dr. Michael Resnick at the University of Minnesota indicates that the more teenagers feel loved by their parents, the less likely they are to have early sexual activity, smoke, abuse alcohol or drugs or commit violence or suicide.

Showing Support for Your Kids

Parenting should be fun. When you enjoy your children you demonstrate a positive attitude toward life, and in doing so, become a positive role model for your children. Find time to get involved in the things your children are interested in. This kind of involvement brings everyone in the family closer together, builds relationships, and creates memories that all the

157

members of the family can treasure. Our idea of fun often differs tremendously from that of our kids. Trish Magee, author of *Raising a Happy, Confident, Successful Child* says, "...parents set up activities to do with their children that end up being more work than fun."¹ Becoming involved with your children in their activities, isn't about the event, it's about spending time with your child. Get your child's input.

In our home, we have made it a priority to participate in our children's activities, whatever they may be. We allow our children to tell us what is important to them, so that when we participate with them, they will have a positive experience. For instance, as parents of athletes, we are often called upon to work in different capacities at games or during school activities. Our kids were very adamant about how we must look and dress when we show up at the events, just in case someone realizes we're their parents. It's important to them that we don't embarrass them by looking like "old hags", so they go to great lengths to keep us current - and we humbly comply.

For some reason, when we become parents it seems like we forget what it was like to be a young person. We forget how much it meant to have our parents' stamp of approval on the things we did. Consequently, we've begun raising children who look to

every other source for approval, rather than to their parents. I vividly remember my high school years. I was involved in every sport they would allow (mostly just to stay after school). What remained in my memory most was that my activities were never very important to my parents. Other parents came to every game and cheered for their kids. They got to know the other kids. They had us over for pizza after the games. Their participation communicated their love and support for their child. It let us know that they were interested in their child's life, not just their grades.

A recent article in the *Better Homes and Gardens* Magazine stated that parents regularly seen on the sidelines are giving up their time. That lets a child know he or she is needed (Better Homes & Gardens, Oct. 1988). "Coming to my game", was the number one answer given in a recent survey conducted with 47 high school juniors and seniors, when asked what their parents did to give them the confidence to make smart choices. Making the effort to be present for a child's victories and milestones is vitally important.

I made a vow to myself long ago that as a parent I would be my child's biggest fan in whatever they attempted. Our son has been a fantastic athlete ever since he could walk, and one of our daughters is a cheerleader. We go to almost every game; all the kids and other parents expect to see us. We dress in the school colors, we cheer the loudest and we get to know the other young people by name. As a result, when other kids are trying to get away from their parents, ours are inviting us along.

Involvement in Sports and Other Activities

Experts say that the most successful young people are ones who earn good grades, are leaders among their peers, strive to succeed in whatever they do, and are involved in sports or other extracurricular activities.

A 1995 study, by the American Social Health Association, concluded that almost 70 percent of 12th graders have had sex (27 percent with four or more partners). This same study showed that high-schoolers who participated in some form of extracurricular activity were less likely to become drug users, be involved in an illegal or violent acts, or participate in premarital sex.

Participating in extracurricular activities not only boosts self-esteem in young people, but it gives them an opportunity to develop positive relationships and helps them to become more disciplined and focused for the future. Most college admissions criteria and recruitment are now focusing more on a students all-around accomplishments, rather than strictly grade point averages. Studies have shown that employers consider their most productive employees to be those who were achievers in a variety of areas, not just academics.

160

School

Some kids seem to be born focused and organized, with exceptional study habits. For those of us who have "normal" children, there is hope! The encouragement and participation of parents can provide a foundation so any student can become an excellent student. A study was conducted 17 years ago following the lives of 81 Illinois students who graduated at the top of their class. They found that these students experienced success in school,

and not in life, because they were hardworking and persistent, not because of any innate talent. Where did the idea of hard work and persistence come from? Parents who demonstrated through their lifestyle that persistence pays off. Jan Won, acting principal of a gifted and talented program in New York City's Chinatown says that "Parents play an essential part as role models...the best students have parents who have responded to their curiosity, nourished and supported the things they were interested in and opened up their world.

Becoming involved in your child's school work can almost be intimidating, especially if we have not remained lifelong learners. As parents we must incorporate learning into everyday life. Our children should see us reading, working through problems, and learning from our mistakes. Make it a point to know what's going on in the classroom. You may not be knowledgable in every subject, but at least know how to help your child find the answers they need. Encourage your children to do their best; to complete against themselves by setting new goals and striving to reach

161

them. This will encourage them while keeping their motivation, performance and self-esteem intact.

Our oldest daughter, Nikki, came to live with us two years ago. When she came at the beginning of the second semester, she had already missed 38 days of school and was failing every class. We knew immediately that we could not associate Nikki's school performance  with who she was as a person or what she was capable of accomplishing in life. We began the second half by setting goals. All "A's" would have been unreasonable and demotivating, so we simply challenged Nikki to compete against herself, to work hard, and expect to see a difference. When the first marking period came we met with Nikki's teachers. She had brought her average up to a "C-". To her teachers, who hadn't known her prior years performance, her grades were discouraging, but for us she had successfully accomplished her goals. This year, Nikki's grades have exceeded our other two children. She's now on the cheerleading squad, on the student counsel, and preparing to go to college.

They key to student success is working to improve skills, not just for the grade. Parents can create a challenging environment for their children to learn and do well in school by being life-long learners themselves. They also need to be aware of what is going on in the classroom and use their wisdom and experience as a resource for their child.

"Love Builds" - Mary McLeod Bethune

Love is the most solid foundation that you can build a relationship with your children on. Foster love by participating in your child's life. The memories and successes that are created through the activities you and your children have shared together will last through generations.

 **Idea File**

⛿ GO TO THEIR GAME
ATTEND GAMES AND OTHER ACTIVITIES AND EVENTS THAT YOUR KIDS ARE INVOLVED IN.

⛿ SET GOALS WITH YOUR CHILDREN
SETTING CLEAR, ACHIEVABLE GOALS PREPARE YOUR KIDS FOR SUCCESS.

⛿ LISTEN TO YOUR CHILD
THE #1 COMPLAINT FOR TEENAGERS IN AMERICA IS THAT THEIR PARENTS DON'T LISTEN TO THEM.

Groom Their Room

23

"Bold colors, lively fabrics and fun designs create a special place where a kid can be a kid."

-Stacia Pierce

In developing extraordinary kids you want to foster an environment that is stable while at the same time stimulating, responsive and loving. The quality of this environment plus social interaction will have a long lasting impact on a child's well being and ability to learn. I can remember when I was fifteen years old and my parents finally gave into the idea of me moving from my former room into the big guest room, and allowing me to design the room as I chose for my birthday present. I had a black and white tiled floor put in, the walls painted starch white with red valances, over black blinds and added the neatest art deco accessories I could find. It was the best gift my parents could of ever gave me., because I fell in love with my room. I began to spend a great deal of time their studying, learning, discovering and dreaming. My high school years were very productive and I contribute a part of that to living in such a colorful, creative environment.

"When children feel they possess their room, the room speaks to them." Says designer Goldbalt. When you allow your kids, that are old enough to help decorate their rooms, they take ownership of their space. If you want to design a child's room for growth then it should be playful, yet sophisticated.

That way if you live in the house for a long length of time the room won't be too babyish after a few years. The main goal you want to achieve in grooming your kids' room is to make the kids room a special space.

The first thing that comes to mind when I think about decorating a child's room is color. Lively, bright colors add a cheerfulness to any environment. We can brighten our kids' rooms by adding color, painting the walls, adding border paper or wall paper, adding colorful draperies or valances, area rugs and bedding. Usually older kids have favorite colors and you should take that into consideration when sprucing up their room.

Most parents want their kids to take pride in their rooms by keeping them neat and clean and putting everything away neatly, but if the parent doesn't help create the right environment it will be very difficult for a child to take pride in his bedroom. Mixmatched sheets, bed spreads, curtains from the fifty's and dressers from grandmas' attic that have not been updated will not motivate a child to want to linger in their room. If the parent won't take pride in their kid's bedroom neither will the child.

Proper storage containers for toys, videos, clothes, dolls, books, etc., should be provided so that everything has a specific place to be stored. Objects of desire should have a place in the kids' room. Things like teddy bears, barbies, books has a specific place to be stored.

Things like teddy bears, barbies, books, their coin collections, stamp collection, Beanie babies collection or for older teens- photos of friends, posters of their favorite singing artist, etc. should also have special storage.

Even if children share a room, there should be separate shelving space or some place in the room that each child can have ownership of their space. You can help your children decorate their rooms very inexpensively. Try using photographs from a recent vacation or a family activity and sit it on their dresser; Frame your children's art work or drawings and put it up in their room. Go through a magazine with your kids and have them create a collage of things they like and make a big poster to put up on the wall.

I bought Ariana a book called *Groom Your Room* from the American Girl Library. She took the book and came up with her own ideas to decorate her room. It's an excellent book for girls ages 8 and up. Too often budget and time constraints push a decorating project for a kids' room to the bottom of the priority list, yet a few simple changes can transform a child's room into a special place. I want to fill my home and my children's bedrooms with love. I do little things for my children to show them I care. I put fresh flowers in vases in my children's rooms and bathrooms and at first they hardly noticed, but now they welcome the touch of freshness that flowers bring into their room.

Sometimes I leave little motivational notes on Ariana's night stand that she can read when she wakes up in the morning. You can create your own little rituals to help fill your children's room with love. It will give them more security.

Speaking of security, you want your children to feel safe in their bedroom. If they have a hard time sleeping at night in their room, go through their bedroom and see if there's anything disturbing. It could be a bad book that got slipped in, an image from a stuffed animal or maybe you just need to add a night light to their room or the hallway.

Try to make their room an educational environment and if space permits put a bookshelf, a desk and chair in your child's room. Every child should have his or her own personal library, to put their book collection. Proper lighting is very important. You need bright lights in a child's room so they don't have to strain to read or play in a dim room. Light adds inspiration and alertness.

Older children need to have their own tape recorders and CD players so they can listen to their music and inspirational tapes in their room. Get them headphones so they don't have to invade anyone else's privacy.

Buy good tapes for your children to listen to. Get tapes from your church so your youth can hear Sunday's lessons again during the week. Right now Ariana is going through the entire Bible by tape. She listens to a tape every night.

A few years ago we read through her Bible in a year by using her one year teen devotional Bible. You will be amazed at how many extraordinary things you can do with your kids in just a short period of time. Once you have all your tools in place the process becomes easy.

 ## Idea File

🏠 LOOK IN YOUR CHILDREN'S ROOM. WHAT DO YOU SEE THAT NEEDS IMPROVING?

🏠 BUY YOUR KIDS STATIONARY BOXES, PENCIL HOLDERS, CD BOXES AND BOOKS SHELVES SO THEY CAN ORGANIZE THEIR ROOMS.

🏠 YOUR CHILDREN'S CLOSETS SHOULD HAVE ORDER. MATCHING HANGERS GIVE A CRISP LOOK. CLOTHES CATEGORIZED BY PANTS, SHIRTS, SKIRTS, DRESSES ETC., MAKE IT SIMPLE FOR YOUR CHILDREN TO DRESS.

🏠 CHECK THE LIGHTING IN YOUR KIDS' ROOM CAN, THEY STUDY OR READ BY IT?

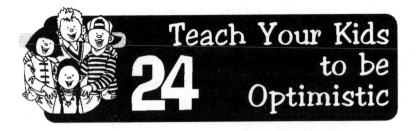

Teach Your Kids to be Optimistic

24

"Protect your kids' enthusiasm from the negativity of others."
-Stacia Pierce

Optimism for kids is stimulated by the environment in which they live. That's why it's essential to strive to make your home a fun, loving and inspiring place that is full of energy. You can control and limit the amount of pessimistic behavior that infiltrates into your home. William Hazlitt said, **"If you think you can win, you can win. Faith is necessary to victory."**

The TV, sad musical lyrics and even negative people can cause a pessimistic environment in your home. For the next week do a check around your house. Observe your kids and determine if you have been allowing too much negativity into your home.

Optimistic children thrive better in life and accomplish more than their peers. Optimism spreads. It's very contagious and inviting. An optimistic child will obtain favor from both his or her peers as well as from adults. Optimistic kids have better relationships and more friends. Optimism causes people to gravitate toward you. Encourage optimism on a consistent basis.

10 Ways To Raise Optimistic Kids

1. Monitor Their Friendships

Children need friends who will affirm and support them. They also need to provide affirmation and support for others.

Help your kids to be good friends by teaching them:

* To give compliments to their friends.
* That the more they give, the more they get back.
* To appreciate the difference in others.
* Not to gossip.
* Not to be a bully. Explain that no one wants to be pushed around or controlled.
* To strive to get along with others.

2. Color their World

Brighten their bedrooms with the proper lighting. Add color to walls, windows, sheets, bedspreads, carpet and posters in their bedrooms. Place fresh flowers in colored vases in the bathroom that they use.

3. Buy Updated Music

Fill your home with cheerful, positive, uplifting music.

4. Affirm Them

Daily speak affirming words to each of your children. Build up their self-esteem. Show enthusiasm about your life and your home environment. Laugh a lot with your kids.

172

"The cheerful man will do more in the same time, will do it better, will preserve it longer than the sad or sullen."

— **Winston Churchill**

5. Be A Positive Role Model

Since children learn the most by imitating, they need models rather than critics. Think about your own attitude. Are you always having a problem or crisis? Do you complain a lot? Do they hear you on the phone being negative about your circumstances? Assess yourself.

6. Buy them Optimistic Books

I bought a book for my daughter called *"Making the Most of Today"*, by Pamela Espeland & Rosemary Wallren.[1] It has daily readings for young people on self awareness, creativity and self-esteem . I encourage my daughter to read a page every day before she goes to school.

7. Invest in Quote Books

In the children's bathroom I keep *Kid's Little Instruction Book* by Jim & Steve Dobson. In this little book many child related actors and authors as well as presidents have their quotes for kids on success and achievement. By keeping optimistic material around your house it also shows that you value optimism. For young kids ages 3-8 try *God's Little Instruction Book for Kids* by Honor Books.

8. Have Your Kids Write A Happy List

I invested in a write in book called *14,000 Things for Kids to be Happy About* by Barbara Ann Kipfer. The book gives kids idea starters and then they have to complete the list. For example, it says: things to be happy about: my family, summer, school, sports, my body and so on. It's a great tool to stir up optimistic thinking.

9. Guard their Mouth

When you notice your kids being hard on themselves, speaking poorly about a friend, saying negative things to their siblings, or continually exaggerating situations with doom and gloom, stop them and cause them to recognize what they are saying and how pessimistic it sounds.

10. Help Them Discover The Bright Side

When your children are being negative about a situation, present a bright side. Explaining things may not always go as planned, but you can get a victory out of the outcome.

 **Idea File**

FOR ONE WEEK OBSERVE THE OPTIMISM LEVEL IN YOUR HOME. EVERY TIME YOU CATCH ONE OF YOUR CHILDREN BEING PESSIMISTIC, CORRECT THEM AND CHALLENGE THEM TO THINK ON THE BRIGHT SIDE.

Have Extraordinary Birthday Parties

25

"The difference between ordinary and extraordinary is that little 'extra'"

- Author Unknown

Birthday parties are an excellent way to introduce your children to a new phase in their life or emphasize something your children love. Birthdays can be a time you can create an occasion to be remembered. With a little creative imagination you can turn an ordinary occasion into an extraordinary event.

When we take time to make beautiful presentations for our children, the gesture sends a message of love to them. Last year Ariana had a very formal tea party. This year my theme for Ariana's birthday was entitled "Ariana's Success Story" The whole concept was based on Ariana learning the importance of self improvement. A few months prior to Ariana's birthday, I began to give a lot of thought to what things she needed in her life right then. Ideas began to come to me here and there, like increase her personal reading time. For one month, I would share a lesson with her every evening about personal body care and self-esteem. Then early one morning after my prayer time, it dawned on me what I could do to make Ariana's life a success story. A flood of ideas came to me. I saw file folders, agendas, and calling cards as decorative pieces for her birthday.

I wrote out the entire plan for her birthday and went to work. There were seven girls invited to her party. For each girl I had personal calling cards made, listing their hobbies, favorite color, phone number, street address and e-mail address. Then I went shopping for file folders. Each girl received five folders, stacked in a plastic file tray along with a business card holder. Next I found plastic, florescent pink briefcases for each girl, which were on their seats when they arrived at the party. I bought foam board and sparkling letters and created a sign which said, " Ariana's Executive Suite". I borrowed an eight foot long table which served as the girls board room table and of course Ariana had the big, high back chair. I made place mats that said "Ariana Inc." and had them laminated.

Karen Mains said, "Don't be afraid to do things with flair...Flair is a creative expression God has imprinted on our souls."

I bought each girl a phone book that had a place for photographs. We took Polaroid photo's of each girl at the party and filled in the phone books before they left. The cake was custom made to look like a pink briefcase. The girls were so excited, and they expressed their appreciation for learning so much at the birthday party. Not only did I introduce Ariana to a new phase in her life, but I also introduced her closest friends (those in her circle of influence) as well.

We have to do uncommon things for our children if we want them to grow up and be uncommon adults. H. Hoover said it well, *"It is a curious fact that when you get sick you want an uncommon doctor; if your car breaks down , you want an uncommonly good mechanic; when we get into war we dreadfully want an uncommon admiral or an uncommon general. I have never met a father and mother who did not want their children to grow up to be uncommon men and women. May it always be so. For the future of America rests not in mediocrity, but in the constant renewal of leadership, in every phase of our national life."*

Use "uncommon" events to add to the lives of your children. Regardless of the cost, time and work, create special celebrations to mark great times with your family. It is worth the effort to provide your kids with many fun-filled memories of their childhood, and build traditions that will continue for years to come. Because every gathering, birthday, holiday and party creates a portion of your family history, it is important that they are all well-planned and loads of fun. Remember, the years move quickly, so go the extra mile to add a little spice to the lifestyle of your loved-ones.

 **Idea File**

HERE ARE THE AGENDAS AND FORMS THAT WERE CREATED FOR ONE OF ARIANA'S BIRTHDAY PARTIES. HOPEFULLY THEY WILL GIVE YOU SOME GREAT IDEAS FOR THE NEXT PARTY YOU HOST.

Ariana's Office Memo:

Friday February 12, 1999

Welcome to ARIANA INC.

Today you will experience the wonderful world of business and learn some fun ways to be a success. Get ready for all the exciting things on your "To Do" List!

Your "To Do" List:

1. Networking Dinner

Explain your career and describe your day at work. This is your chance to exchange business cards.

2. Company I.D. Cards

So that you are recognized as a CEO, we will take pictures and create your identification cards for future business projects.

3. Desktop Discovery

A fun memory game featuring office tools.

4. The "Marketing Me" Project

You will develop an "I Like Me" Poster for the Marketing Dept.
Design 6 scenes describing your day at work
* Remember the most important product to market is you!

5. Filing Fun with Ariana

As officers of Ariana Inc., you have a meeting with the Vice President Shar Starr, who will show you how to make *Dream Files*. During the meeting, you will learn to collect stuff like, articles, newspaper and magazine clips to show things you want to have and give information about what you want to become.

Business Bonus
Treasure Hunt

Read the Hints Below and Find Your Treasure!

1. Doll for the Deal:
Congratulations! You closed the deal with Mattel. We left a
special b--b-- doll somewhere in the lower level.

2. What a Winner Writes With:
For your outstanding commitment to the company, we
have a really cool pen for you to find.

3. The Buying Game:
Ariana Inc. has recently purchased "Boardwalk", "Park Place", and
"Pennsylvania Ave." find the box that contains
the deed cards, and money.

4. Get In Shape Surprise:
You will get a real "workout" trying to find this book."

5. Hidden for your Hair:
Decorate your hair with these items to hold your hair
and keep it "tight!"

*Created exclusively for Ariana Inc.

Hey, You're Invited to

Part 2
Company Party

PARTY PLANS:

Special Presentation
We have a special presentation of gifts for the CEO Ariana Pierce

Dessert
Strawberry Torte Cake & Ice Cream for everyone!

Break to the Executive Washroom:
Bathe & Relax in your pajamas in our luxurious accomodations

Charades for CEO's
An awesome game to "show" your favorite career

Business Bonus Treasure Hunt
Find great corporate goodies all over the executive suite

Briefcase Boogie
Search the briefcase, put on your business attire, boogie to your favorite Christian hits, then take a glamour shot

Media Center Movies
All company employees join us in the theater for movies

Retire to your Suite
Get settled in for a good night's rest

*Hosted for Ariana Inc.

Desktop Discovery

1.
2.
3.
4.
5.
6.
7.
8.
9.
10.
11.
12.
13.
14.
15.
16.
17.
18.
19.
20.   *Created exclusively for Ariana Inc.

Ariana's
Morning Memo:
Saturday February 13, 1999

Your "To Do" List:

1. Executive Breakfast
Join your business buddies for a tasty meal

2. Project Filo Fax
Create a personalized phone book with photos of your friends

3. Working Woman's Makeovers
Free Makeovers complimentary of Ariana Inc.

4. Professional Postcards Design Club
Join the design team and create cool postcards telling
a friend or family member about the fun you had at the
Success Story Birthday Party.

Thank you for coming!

*Created exclusively for Ariana Inc

Other Extraordinary Tips:

★ Know your children's friends

★ Kiss your children good-night, even if they are already asleep.

★ Invest in your children's dreams

★ Collect excellent reference books and resources that support your child's interest.

★ Be a buyer of empty books for your kids. Invest in journals and writing tools such as pens, pencils markers, colored pencils, etc.

★ Take a close look at your children's bookshelves, music, entertainment and friends. Do those things reflect the values that you want instilled in your children?

★ Buy your kids a dictionary.

★ Play classical music while your kids are studying or doing homework.

★ Pray with your children.

★ Enjoy your children's growing years. Plan a tea party, or picnic just to enjoy each others company.

✺ Believe in your children regardless of their limitations or struggles.

✺ Know your children's teachers, and attend parent/teacher conferences.

✺ Introduce your kids to poetry.

✺ Have a "dream sharing" day with your family.

Notes

#1 Wake Up Your Child's Dream
1. Doodle a Day Calendar by American Girl, (Pleasant Company Aug 1998)

#4 Develop A Personal Growth Plan
1. Richest Man in Babylon, George S. Clayson, (New American Library, reissue 1997)
How to Win Friends and Influence People, Dale Carnegie (Pocket Books 1994 reissue)

#5 Raise A Reader
1. Mary Kate & Ashley Olsen Series, Scholastic Paperbacks
2. Clueless, H.B. Gilmore, Pocket Books (1995)
3. *How to get your Kids Hooked on Books*, Karen O'Conner (Nelson Publishers 1995)

#6 Raise a Writer
1. *All about Me,* Linda Krantz, (Rising Moon, Sept 1996)
2. *My Faith Journal* Karen Hill, (Thomas Nelson 1997)
3. *Amelia's Notebook*, by Marissa Moss, (Pleasant Company Publications Jan 1999)

#9 Teach Money Matters
1. Fortune Magazine Feb 1998
2. Parents Magazine Jan 1998

#11 Provide Ongoing Motivation for your Kids
1. Biography. Family Life. March 1999. pg. 30
2. *Lots of Love in a Lunch Box,* Joy L. Stevens, (Standard Publishing Nov 1998)
4. *The World of William Joyce Scrapbook,* (Haper-Collins Juvenille Books 1997)

#12 Become a Better Mom
1. *Power of a Praying Parent*, Stormie Omartian, (Havest House Publishers July 1995)

#13 Say I Love You
1. *The Five Love Languages of Children*, Gary Chapman, Northfield Publishers 1997
2. I Corinthians 13:4-8a NIV.

#14 Practice Listening
1. *Don't Sweat the Small Stuff...and It's All Small Stuff* (Richard Carlson, Hyperion 1997)

#16 Promote a Good Body Image
1. *The Care And Keeping Of You,* by the American Girls Library (Pleasant company Publications)
2. *"A Christian Woman's Guide to Health and Nutrition",* Stacia Pierce (Life Changers, 1996)
"Food Smart" by Cheryl Townsley, JP Thracher (1997 reprint)
3. Sept. Parent's Magazine 1998. Pg. 44

#19 Take Exciting Vacations and Spend Quality Time Together
My New York by Kathy Jakobsen, (Little Brown & Company Sept. 1993)

#22 Enjoy Activities with Your Kids
1. *Raising a Happy, Confident, Successful Child,* Trish Magee, (Adams Media Corp.)

23 Groom Their Room
1. *Groom Your Room,* The American Girls Library, (Pleasant Company Sept 1997)

24 Teach Your Kids to Be Optimistic
#2 *Making the Most of Today,* Pamela Espland & Rosemary Wallner. (Troll Publishing).

All Scriptures taken from the Holy Bible
The King James Version (KJV)
New International Version (NIV)
New King James Version (NKJV)
or The Living Bible (TLB)

About the Author

Stacia Pierce has a message of optimism that tells women there is greatness in them. Stacia focuses on the possibilities for women instead of the limitations. She illuminates purpose and direction in others and gives them the motivation to live above average.

A popular speaker who travels nationwide for seminars, workshops and conferences; Stacia carries out her mission to train, inspire and lead women to live truly successful lives. Due to her enthusiasm, charisma and ability to communicate with people of all ages, women are compelled to create a life worth living.

Stacia is the author of six books, thirteen leadership manuals, Editor-in-Chief of *W.O.R.D.* Magazine, director of a women's leadership team, on the advisory council of *Aspire* Magazine. founder of *Women in the Word*, as well as the Women's Success Institute and the host of the international Women's Success Conference.

She has a heart for women and anyone exposed to her ministry will have their lives changed forever.

Stacia, her husband Pastor James and their two children: Ryan and Ariana reside in Lansing, MI.

Audio Cassettes by Stacia Pierce

Below is a small sample of the awesome audio cassette teachings Stacia available. To order or to receive a complete listing, please call: 517-333-9860

THE SOCIAL SAVVY SERIES

The Social Savvy Series lessons are packed with power points, quick tips and handy information to equip you to be socially confident.

Item #	Title	Price
SS62	Disciplines of a Happy Home (5)	$25.00
SS63	How to Build Proper Friendships (2)	$10.00
SS64	How to Journalize (2)	$10.00
SS65	Tea Breaks w/ Stacia Pierce (1)	$5.00
SS67	A Woman's Personal Space (1)	$5.00
SS68	How to Celebrate the Seasons (1)	$5.00
SS69	The Art of Taking Care of You	$5.00

Women In The Word

This collection of tape series are great for personal and spiritual growth. Stacia covers topics important to women and provides matter-of-fact, insight to better living.

SS70	The Achievers Notebook	$5.00
W14	How To Build the Life You Want (2)	$10.00
W20	The Power of Positive Words (2)	$10.00
W21	How Prayer Can Change Your Life (1)	$5.00
W23	How to Walk in Divine Favor (1)	$5.00
W24	How to Have Enjoyment & Fulfillment in Your Marriage (1)	$5.00

THE *Women's* SUCCESS AUDIO CLUB

It's the audio magazine you've been waiting for! Get your subscription today. Each month Stacia shares a motivational message with practical solutions to life's challenges. With the Women's Audio Club you will gain a balanced comprehensive approach to creating your success.

C5	Frame Your Future (1)	$6.00
C6	Getting Great Ideas (1)	$6.00
C7	How to Look & Feel Like a Million (1)	$6.00
C10	Great Agendas for Good Success (1)	$6.00
C14	How to Live a Rewarding Life (1)	$6.00

WSI

The Women's Success Institute

STACIA PIERCE, FOUNDER

THE WOMEN'S SUCCESS INSTITUTE (WSI) IS DEDICATED TO TRAINING AND MENTORING CHRISTIAN WOMEN TO BE EQUIPPED TO FULFILL THEIR GOD-GIVEN TASK. WSI IS A PROGRAM OF LIFE CHANGERS CHRISTIAN CENTER, HEADED BY STACIA PIERCE AND WILL OFFER SPECIAL WORKSHOPS FOR WOMEN WHO ARE CHOOSING LEADERSHIP.

SESSIONS SUCH AS *HOW TO WRITE A BOOK*, *HOW TO PREPARE A MESSAGE*, *HOW TO BUILD A WOMEN'S LEADERSHIP TEAM* AND MUCH MORE WILL BE HELD EXCLUSIVELY FOR WSI MEMBERS ONLY. WSI WILL PROVIDE YOU WITH RESOURCES, EDUCATION, TRAINING AND CERTIFICATION TO HELP WOMEN SERVE GOD IN THEIR LOCAL CHURCH, MINISTRY OR PROFESSIONAL CAREERS.

YOU'LL RECEIVE:

A BIMONTHLY NEWSLETTER packed with ideas and information, for women who lead.

SPECIAL DISCOUNT RATES for selected WSI sponsored events and selected materials from Stacia Pierce

PRAYER SUPPORT of Stacia Pierce and the women's leadership team. As a member, you will be under their continual prayer covering

PRIORITY BOOKING with Stacia Pierce.

PARTNERSHIP NETWORKING during the annual Women's Success Conference and other WSI events, will create a strong network of support with other women leaders.

PARTNERSHIP WOMEN'S MINISTRY PACKET full of resources to equip you for leadership.

Women's Success Institute Application

Name: _____

Address: _____

City: _____ State_____ Zip_____

Phone: daytime # :(_____)_____-_____

         evening #:(_____)_____

E-mail:_____ Fax: (_____)_____

Church Name:_____

Church Address: _____

City: _____ State_____ Zip_____

Ministry Position: _____

or Job Title (if applicable): _____

What do you need most from Stacia Pierce and the **WSI**? Explain:

_____

_____

_____

_____

_____

_____

What leadership roles are you already actively involved in?

_____

_____

_____

_____

To become a lifetime member of the Women's Success Institute and receive my **WSI** Portfolio Packet loaded with informative "tip sheets." simply send **$49.95** along with this completed form to:

Life Changers Christian Center
808 Lake Lansing Road Ste. 200
East Lansing, MI 48823
517-333-9860

The Women's SUCCESS Audio Club
with STACIA PIERCE

MOTIVATIONAL TEACHING BY STACIA PIERCE, WITH PRACTICAL SOLUTIONS AND LIFE CHANGING INFORMATION. STACIA WILL CAUSE YOU TO EXPAND YOUR VISION, IMPROVE YOUR MINISTRY SKILLS AND INSPIRE YOU TO HAVE SUCCESS WITH GOD!

SPECIAL BONUS WOMEN'S BOOKCLUB NEWSLETTER: STACIA WILL KEEP YOU UP TO DATE AND INFORMED BY PROVIDING YOU WITH BOOKS AND RESOURCES THAT WILL CHANGE YOUR LIFE.

GET IDEAS THAT WILL CAUSE YOU TO EXCEL IN YOUR HOME, RELATIONSHIPS AND MINISTRY.

SIGN UP TODAY AND RECEIVE THE MOST AWESOME SUCCESS PRINCIPLES FOR DAILY LIVING THAT YOU'VE EVER HEARD.

TO ORDER YOUR 12 MONTH SUBSCRIPTION, SIMPLY COMPLETE THE INFORMATION BELOW, ENCLOSE **$69.95** AND SEND TO:

LIFE CHANGERS CHRISTIAN CENTER
808 LAKE LANSING ROAD STE. 200
EAST LANSING, MI 48823
517-333-9860

Name:_____

Address:_____

City:_____ State:_____ Zip:_____

Phone: Day (   )_____ Evening (   )_____

Payment Method: ❑cash   ❑check   ❑money order   ❑credit card

❑Master Card   ❑VISA   ❑American Express   ❑Discover

Card#:_____ Exp. Date_____

Cardholder's signature_____

OTHER BOOKS BY STACIA PIERCE

THE CHRISTIAN WOMEN'S GUIDE TO HEALTH AND NUTRITION

25 WAYS WOMEN CAN MOTIVATE THEMSELVES

25 WAYS ORDINARY WOMEN CAN LIVE EXTRAORDINARY LIVES

THE SUCCESS SECRETS OF A READER

THE PRAYER & PURPOSE PLANNER

I'd love to hear from you. I invite you to share your thoughts and comments concerning this book. Please write me.

Fondly, Stacia

TO RECEIVE MORE INFORMATION ABOUT ADDITIONAL MATERIALS BY STACIA PIERCE, OR ENGAGE HER FOR SEMINARS, OR WOMEN'S CONFERENCES, PLEASE CALL OR WRITE:

LIFE CHANGERS CHRISTIAN CENTER
808 LAKE LANSING ROAD SUITE 200
EAST LANSING, MI 48823
517-333-9860